DK EYEWITNESS

WITHDRAWN

TOP 10
ISTANBUL

Top 10 Istanbul Highlights

The Top 10 of Everything

CONTENTS

Istanbul Area by Area

Streetsmart

Within each Top 10 list in this book, no hierarchy of quality or popularity is implied. All 10 are, in the editor's opinion, of roughly equal merit.

Title page, front cover and spine
The church of Haghia Sophia at daybreak
Back cover, clockwise from top left *Ceramics in the Grand Bazaar; view from Galata Tower at sunset; the famous Spice Bazaar; Haghia Sophia; street facing Galata Tower at night*

Welcome to
Istanbul

Istanbul is unique. No other city straddles two continents. No other city has been capital of two mighty empires. Its venerable churches, mosques and palaces do justice to its incredible past. This teeming metropolis of 15 million has a vibrant present, too, as a hotbed of the arts, and a shoppers', clubbers' and foodies' paradise. With Eyewitness Top 10 Istanbul, it is yours to explore.

The city is defined by the sea. Imagine hopping across the **Bosphorus Strait** for lunch in Asia; gazing out at the Sea of Marmara from the rooftop of your Sultanahmet hotel; or watching the exotic mosque-filled skyline of the Old City unfold as you go up the **Golden Horn** on a ferry. Istanbul is a city of contrasts, too. The ancient cathedral of **Haghia Sophia** is breathtaking; so is the **Istanbul Modern** gallery. Wander the backstreets of devout Fatih among bearded acolytes from the *medreses* by day; at night sip a cocktail in a chic rooftop bar in **Beyoğlu**, the heart of modern European Istanbul.

It isn't just the Bosphorus that divides Istanbul. The **Old City** sits on a hilly peninsula pointing at Asia. Here, Byzantine monuments, Ottoman mosques, historic markets such as the **Grand Bazaar**, and venerable **Turkish baths** predominate. Across the Golden Horn in Galata and Beyoğlu, three million shoppers, diners, and bar and gallery hoppers throng **İstiklal Caddesi**, on any given weekend.

Whether you're visiting for a weekend or a week, our Top 10 guide brings together the best of everything the city has to offer, from the best Turkish cuisine to the most magnificent historic monuments. The guide has useful tips throughout, from seeking out what's free to avoiding the crowds, plus eight, easy-to-follow itineraries, designed to tie together a clutch of sights in a short space of time. Add inspiring photography and detailed maps, and you've got the essential pocket-sized travel companion. **Enjoy the book, and enjoy Istanbul**.

Clockwise from top: **Haghia Sophia, Blue Mosque, Basilica Cistern, Rumeli Hisarı Fortress, Eyüp Sultan Mosque, the Galata Tower and Golden Horn, Great Palace Mosaic Museum**

Exploring Istanbul

With so much to see and do in this continent-straddling city, it's sometimes hard to know where to begin. In order to help you make the most of your time, here are a few ideas for two and four days of sightseeing in Istanbul.

| 0 metres | 1000 |
| 0 yards | 1000 |

Haghia Sophia's massive dome is considered to be the epitome of Byzantine architecture.

Two Days in Istanbul

Day ❶

MORNING

Admire the soaring dome and glittering mosaics of **Haghia Sophia** (see pp16–17), then head off to explore the vast **Blue Mosque** (see pp18–19).

AFTERNOON

Visit the sprawling **Topkapı Palace** (see pp12–15), the nerve-centre of the Ottoman Empire. Afterwards relax in the **Çemberlitaş Baths** (see pp30–31).

Day ❷

MORNING

Explore the **Archaeological Museum** (see pp20–21), full of artifacts from the Ottoman Empire's former domains.

AFTERNOON

Stroll to the top of the Old City's third hill to the **Süleymaniye Mosque Complex** (see pp26–7), which offers views of the Bosphorus from its terrace. Then head back down to the bustling **Grand Bazaar** (see pp22–3) to weave through its 4,000 shops.

Four Days in Istanbul

Day ❶

MORNING

Spend most of the morning in the Byzantine cathedral of **Haghia Sophia** (see pp16–17), before descending into the eerie depths of the **Basilica Cistern** (see p63).

AFTERNOON

Catch a ferry up the Golden Horn to Ayvansaray and walk the line of the **Theodosian Walls** (see p42) to the fresco-filled wonder of the **Church of St Saviour in Chora** (see pp28–9). Recover in the steaming **Çemberlitaş Baths** (see pp30–31).

Day ❷

MORNING

Start fresh in the airy courtyards and pavilions of the **Topkapı Palace** (see pp12–15) before walking across Sultanahmet Meydan park to the nearby **Blue Mosque** (see pp18–19). Lunch in a tradesman's cafe in the **Grand Bazaar** (see pp22–3).

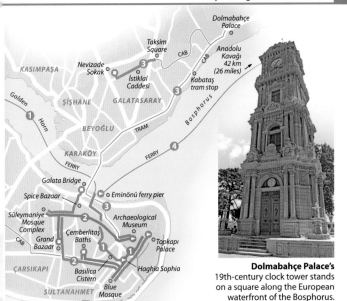

Dolmabahçe Palace's 19th-century clock tower stands on a square along the European waterfront of the Bosphorus.

Key
— Two-day itinerary
— Four-day itinerary

The bustling Eminönü ferry pier viewed from the Galata Bridge.

AFTERNOON

After exploring the bazaar, walk up to **Süleymaniye Mosque Complex** (see pp26–7) then down to the **Spice Bazaar** (see pp70–71) and **Eminönü** (see p70) waterfront. Lunch on a fish sandwich by **Galata Bridge** (see p70).

Day ❸
MORNING

Enjoy the splendours of the **Archaeological Museum** (see pp20–21) before taking a tram across the Golden Horn to Kabataş, then a cab or bus to the opulent, Baroque-style **Dolmabahçe Palace** (see pp32–3), home to the later Ottoman sultans.

AFTERNOON

After exploring Dolmabahçe Palace, take a cab up to **Taksim Square** (see p84). Walk down the city's premier shopping and entertainment street, **İstiklal Caddesi** (see p86), and enjoy a meal at a lively *meyhane* (tavern) on **Nevizade Sokak** (see p89).

Day ❹
ALL DAY

Around 10:30am, depart from the Eminönü ferry pier on the all-day **Bosphorus Cruise** (see pp34–5). Enjoy fantastic views of the city's shoreline before lingering over a fish lunch in **Anadolu Kavağı** (see p94).

Top 10 Istanbul Highlights

The monumental Byzantine church
of Haghia Sophia

🔟 Istanbul Highlights

Inhabited for at least 8,000 years, Istanbul was the capital of two of the world's most powerful empires – the Byzantines and the Ottomans – and its every stone is steeped in history. The highlights are easy; you can cover the major attractions in the first couple of days. But after that, the choice can be overwhelming, especially as this ancient city is reinventing itself once more as a modern centre for nightlife, food and shopping. The only answer is to come back again and again to this endlessly fascinating city.

① Topkapı Palace

A palace fit for a sultan, the Topkapı was not only a royal residence, but also the Ottoman Empire's centre of government (see pp12–15).

② Haghia Sophia

One of the most revered icons of the Christian church, Haghia Sophia has stood for 1,500 years – a miraculous feat of design and engineering that has out-lived two great empires (see pp16–17).

③ Blue Mosque

Sultan Ahmet I's stunningly impressive mosque is one of the world's most famous religious buildings. "Blue" on account of the delicately patterned İznik tiles that adorn the interior (see pp18–19).

④ Archaeological Museum

Turkey's world-class national collection contains ancient treasures from across the Ottoman Empire and beyond, including artifacts from Babylon, Syria, Egypt, Greece, Rome and Persia (see pp20–21).

Süleymaniye Mosque Complex ⑥

Sultan Süleyman I built this magnificent mosque to glorify Allah and his own rule. The architect was the exceptional Sinan, who designed over 400 buildings throughout the empire *(see pp26–7)*.

⑤ Grand Bazaar

The Grand Bazaar remains a true delight, a shopaholic's fantasy that is also a photographer's dream *(see pp22–3)*.

⑦ Church of St Saviour in Chora

With more than 100 early-14th-century mosaics and frescoes, this church is one of the city's most important Byzantine treasures *(see pp28–9)*.

Çemberlitaş Baths ⑧

Relaxing beneath the marble domes of these traditional baths offers a cleansing, cultural and reviving experience *(see pp30–31)*.

⑨ Dolmabahçe Palace

This 19th-century Occidental fantasy was commissioned by Sultan Abdül Mecit. The decision to build this opulent palace almost bankrupted the Treasury, and in the end could be financed only by foreign loans *(see pp32–3)*.

⑩ Bosphorus Cruise

Take to the water on a ferry trip up the Bosphorus. The air is clean, the pace unhurried and, best of all, sightseeing can be done from the deck *(see pp34–5)*.

★ Topkapı Palace

Fresh from his conquest of Constantinople, Mehmet II built Topkapı Sarayı as his main residence between 1460 and 1478. He planned it as a series of pavilions in four courtyards – a tribute in stone to the tent encampments of his nomadic forebears. Mehmet's palace was also the seat of government, and had a college for training officials and soldiers. While government moved across the road to the Sublime Porte in the 16th century, Topkapı continued as the sultan's palace until Abdül Mecit I moved to Dolmabahçe Palace in 1856.

1 Imperial Gate
(Bâb-ı Hümayun)
Built in 1478, this gate is the main entrance to the palace. Gatekeepers' quarters are on either side. An apartment belonging to Mehmet II above the gate was destroyed by fire in 1866.

The picturesque Topkapı Palace

2 Harem
A maze of rooms and corridors **(above)**, the Harem was a closed world occupied by the sultan's wives, concubines and children.

3 First Courtyard
(Alay Meydanı)
This vast outer courtyard takes in Gülhane Park, Sirkeci, the church *(see p43)* of Haghia Eirene (Aya Irini Kilisesi) and the imposing Archaeological Museum.

4 Gate of Salutations
(Bâb-üs Selâm)
At this elaborate gate **(left)**, built in 1524, visitors were greeted, and high officials who had upset the sultan were arrested and beheaded. The gateway leads into the Second Courtyard (Divan Meydanı), where the Treasury now has a magnificent display of arms and armour.

5 Kitchens
These huge kitchens once catered for 1,000 people a day. On display is a collection of ceramics **(left)**, crystal and silver, including the Chinese celadon ware favoured by early sultans.

6 Throne Room
(Arz Odası)
In the Throne Room **(below)**, the Sultan consulted his ministers and governors, welcomed ambassadors and other dignitaries, and hosted smaller state occasions.

Topkapı Palace

10 Imperial Sofa (Sofa-ı-Hümayun)

The Imperial Sofa **(below)** was a place to relax, its gardens studded with pavilions built by successive sultans. The finest is the Baghdad Pavilion (Bağdat Köşkü).

7 Third Courtyard (Enderûn Meydanı)

The Gate of Felicity (Bâb-üs Saadet) leads to the Third Courtyard, containing the sultan's private quarters and those of the Harem's white eunuchs.

8 Imperial Wardrobe (Seferli Koğuşu)

The Imperial Wardrobe is now the home of the costume museum, a collection of some 3,000 embroidered royal robes. It is under construction and is due to reopen in 2020.

9 Treasury (Hazine Koğuşu)

With exhibits including the jewel-encrusted Topkapı Dagger and the amazing 86-carat Spoonmaker's Diamond **(right)**, the Treasury may be the most ostentatious collection of wealth ever gathered outside of the legendary Aladdin's cave.

Features of the Topkapı Harem

1 Barracks of the Black Eunuchs

Apart from the sultan and his sons, the only men allowed into the Harem were the African eunuchs, up to 200 slaves from Sudan and Ethiopia. Their barracks lie on one side of the Courtyard of the Black Eunuchs, with its arcade of marble columns.

Courtyard of the Concubines

2 Courtyard of the Concubines

This colonnaded courtyard lies beside the Harem Baths. As many as 300 concubines lived in the Harem at any one time.

3 Golden Cage

Mehmet III became sultan in 1595, following the murder of all but one of his 19 brothers. After that, heirs to the throne were kept in the "Golden Cage", a secure area of the Harem, until they were needed. As a result, many were weak and ill-fitted for rule when they took the throne.

4 Wives' Apartments

The sultan's wives (under Islamic law, he was allowed four) also had their own apartments. While wives took formal precedence in the Harem hierarchy, the real power lay with the sultan's favourites and mother. Occasionally, a sultan would marry a concubine – as in the case of Süleyman I, who married his beloved Roxelana (known in Turkish as Haseki Hürrem).

5 Salon of the Valide Sultan

The *valide sultan* (sultan's mother) was by far the most powerful woman in the palace, and enjoyed the use of some of the best rooms in the Harem.

6 Sultan's Apartments

The sultan spent much of his off-duty time in his suite within the Harem. Look out for the bedroom of Sultan Abdül Hamit I (1774–89), the Hall of Murat III (1574–95) and the beautiful Fruit Room.

7 Imperial Baths

Next to each other at the centre of the complex are the baths of the sultan and the *valide sultan*, both elegantly faced with marble.

8 Imperial Hall

In the Imperial Hall, the sultan entertained his closest friends. Although the hall was within the Harem, only a few women – the sultan's mother, chief wife, favourites and daughters – were allowed entry.

9 Favourites' Apartments

Haseki (favourites) who bore a child received their own apartments and their freedom (if slaves). After the sultan's death, those who had borne only daughters were moved to the old palace or married out of the Harem; those with sons stayed in the palace.

Favourites' Apartments

10 Golden Way

This long, dark passage was so called because, on festivals, the Sultan would scatter gold coins here for the members of the Harem.

LIFE IN THE HAREM

Behind the doors of the Harem, life was far less exciting than it was portrayed to be in the breathless accounts of 19th-century European commentators. There was undoubtedly intrigue and, if a woman was fortunate enough to be one of the sultan's favourites, she might well develop a taste for lavish comfort and lovely gifts, yet daily existence for most was mundane – even dully routine. The Harem was less a den of vice than a family home and girls' school. Of its 1,000 or so occupants, more than two-thirds were servants or royal children, while concubines – who usually arrived between the ages of 5 and 12 – spent many years living in dormitories and undergoing a thorough education before being introduced to the sultan.

Princess Mihrimah (1522–78), the daughter of Süleyman I

TOP 10 OTTOMAN WOMEN

1 Hafsa Sultan (mother of Süleyman I)

2 Roxelana (wife of Süleyman)

3 Nurbanu Sultan (wife of Selim II, daughter-in-law of Süleyman)

4 Mihrimah (daughter of Süleyman, wife of Grand Vizier Rüstem Paşa)

5 Safiye Sultan (mother of Mehmet III)

6 Handan Sultan (wife of Mehmet III)

7 Kösem Sultan (wife of Ahmet I)

8 Turhan Hatice Sultan (mother of Mehmet IV)

9 Nakşidil Sultan (mother of Mahmut II)

10 Bezmialem (wife of Mahmut II, mother of Abdül Mecit I)

Women Drinking Coffee (1720s), by Jean-Baptiste Vanmour, is part of a collection of European art depicting life in the Harem. It is on display in the Pera Museum.

TOP 10 ★ Haghia Sophia

Haghia Sophia, the Church of Holy Wisdom (Ayasofya in Turkish), is an awe-inspiring expression of religious faith and one of the world's foremost architectural wonders. The first church on the site burned down in 404, the second was destroyed during the Nika Riots of 532, but the third – inaugurated by Emperor Justinian in 537 – stands firm today, despite countless wars and earthquakes, a blazing beacon to the faith of its creators. The church was converted into a mosque in 1453. Since 1935, it has been a museum.

1 Exterior
The deep red walls of the exterior are topped by a central dome and flanked by two semi-domes. The main building **(right)** is as it was in the 6th century – except for the buttresses added to secure the structure, which obscure the shape.

2 Galleries
Women used the galleries for prayer. Votive mosaics in the south gallery include Jesus Christ flanked by Empress Zoe and Emperor Constantine IX Monomachus **(below)** and Christ Pantocrator (Almighty) with John the Baptist and the Virgin Mary.

3 Inner Narthex
There are doors leading into the nave from each bay of the inner narthex; the large central one, the Imperial Gate, was once reserved for the emperor and the patriarch. At the south end of the inner narthex, look back above the door as you exit into the Vestibule of the Warriors to see the wonderful late 10th-century mosaic of Constantine and Justinian offering their city and church to the infant Christ.

4 Weeping Pillar
Emperor Justinian rested his aching head against the damp stone of this pillar and was instantly cured. Ever since, visitors have queued to touch the miraculous spot.

5 Columns
The Byzantines were great scavengers, and many of the columns in the Haghia Sophia were probably salvaged from pagan temples.

CHANGING FACES
In the last bay of the south gallery, look for the mosaic of Christ enthroned, flanked by Empress Zoë and Emperor Constantine IX Monomachus. The emperor's head has been altered. Historians believe that the figure was initially a portrait of Zoë's first husband, Romanos III Argyros, but was replaced with the image of her second husband, Michael IV, then the face of her third husband, Constantine.

6 Islamic Elements

The conversion from church to mosque began in 1453. Many of the mosiacs were plastered over, to be rediscovered in the 1930s. The *mihrab* and *minbar* (see p19) were added by Sultan Murat III in the 16th century. Note the calligraphic roundels **(left)** at the dome base.

7 Coronation Square

Set into the floor near the *minbar*, the site of the emperor's throne is marked in a square of patterned marble. In Byzantine times, this was thought to be the centre of the world *(omphalion)*.

8 Nave

On entering the nave **(right)**, the overwhelming impression is of the vast space enclosed by the dome. This sits on four arches rising out of four enormous marble piers, which frame double colonnades at either end.

9 Carpet Museum (Vakıflar Halı Müzesi)

Located behind Haghia Sophia is the old soup kitchen, which today houses some of the country's oldest and finest mosque carpets. The big door of the museum is exemplary of the Baroque architecture in the city.

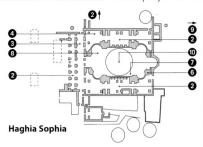

Haghia Sophia

NEED TO KNOW

MAP R4 ■ Sultanahmet Meydanı ■ (0212) 522 17 50 ■ www.ayasofya muzesi.gov.tr

Open mid-Apr–mid-Oct: 9am–7pm Tue–Sun (mid-Oct–mid-Apr: until 5pm)

Adm ₺60; last ticket 1 hour before closing

■ After your visit, it's worth coming back at night to see the exteriors of both Haghia Sophia and the Blue Mosque *(see pp18–19)* floodlit.

■ There is a café located at the western entrance to the complex. There are many options for refreshments in Divanyolu Caddesi *(see p64)*, a short walk away.

10 Dome

The dome **(left)**, 32 m (101 ft) in diameter, rises 56 m (183 ft) above the ground. Supported by 40 ribs made from lightweight hollow bricks, it is a miracle of engineering. The original design survived for 21 years before being destroyed by an earthquake in 1558.

TOP 10 ⭐ Blue Mosque

Sultan Ahmet I was only 19 when he commissioned this mosque, known in Turkish as Sultanahmet Camii. So great was his passion for the project that at times he even worked alongside his labourers. With his architect, Sedefkar Mehmet Ağa, he wanted to surpass the Haghia Sophia and Süleymaniye Mosque Complex (the work of Ağa's teacher, Sinan). The result of their labours, completed in 1616, has become one of the most celebrated mosques in the world, widely known as the Blue Mosque because of the blue İznik tiles inside.

The Setting ①
To underline the supremacy of Islam over Christian Byzantium, the Blue Mosque **(right)** was built opposite Haghia Sophia, on the site of the Byzantine royal palace.

② Entrance
The mosque's main entrance is for practising Muslims only. Separate entrances for visitors of other faiths are around the side of the mosque.

③ Minarets
Legend has it that the sultan asked for a minaret with *altın* (gold), but the architect heard *altı* (six) minarets. The sultan was pleased – at that time no mosque apart from the great mosque in Mecca had six minarets.

④ Domes
Semidomes **(below)** surround the main dome, which is 23.5 m (77 ft) in diameter and 43 m (140 ft) high, and supported by four giant columns, each 5 m (16 ft) in diameter.

⑤ Courtyard
The huge courtyard **(below)**, which is faced with cool marble from the Marmara islands, has the same dimensions as the interior of the prayer hall. Look up for a splendid view of the mosque's cascade of domes and semidomes.

⑥ Ablutions Fountain
The fountain at the centre of the mosque's courtyard is no longer used for ritual ablutions. Instead, the faithful use taps ranged along the outside of the courtyard. Washing the face, arms, neck, feet, mouth and nose is seen as an integral part of the act of prayer.

IZNIK TILES

Ceramic production in İznik began during the Byzantine era. In the early years, the designs were based on Chinese models. Arabic motifs were added by Şah Kulu, one of 16 artists brought in from Tabriz by Sultan Selim I (1512–20). A rich turquoise was added to the traditional blue and white in the 1530s; purples, greens and coral reds came 20 years later. Master designer Kara Memi introduced swirling floral patterns, and by the time Ahmet I placed his order for the Blue Mosque, the İznik style was established.

7 Tiles

There are more than 20,000 blue İznik tiles **(above)** lining the mosque's interior walls. Supplying these tiles put severe pressure on the tile makers, and the sultan banned anyone else from placing orders until his was complete.

8 Minbar and Mihrab

At the front of the mosque are the *minbar* **(below)**, the pulpit from which the imam delivers his sermons, and the *mihrab*, which is a niche that points towards Mecca.

NEED TO KNOW

MAP R5 ■ Sultanahmet Meydanı
■ (0212) 458 49 83

Open 9am–7pm daily (closed at prayer times)

Donations welcome

....

■ To avoid prayer times, make the mosque your first stop in the morning, or visit in the mid-afternoon.

■ There are no places for refreshment inside the mosque complex, but Sultanahmet Square, Divanyolu Caddesi and the Arasta Bazaar offer plenty of possibilities.

9 Sultan's Loge

To the left of the *mihrab* is the galleried box where the sultan prayed. The loge's ceiling is painted with arabesque designs.

10 Carpets

The interior **(left)** of the mosque is laid with a modern carpet. Mosques have always had carpets in order to cushion the knees and forehead during prayer time.

🔟 ⭐ Archaeological Museum

The national collection of one of the world's most ancient countries naturally promises something special, and this fabulous museum does not disappoint. A world-class collection spanning 5,000 years, it was founded in 1881 by Osman Hamdi Bey, the son of a Grand Vizier, fuelled by the realization that European archaeologists and treasure hunters were walking off with much of the Empire's heritage. There are three sections: the main museum, the Tiled Pavilion (Çinili Köşk) and the Museum of the Ancient Orient.

1 Sidon Sarcophagi
Osman Hamdi Bey discovered this remarkable group of 5th- and 4th-century-BC sarcophagi in Sidon (modern-day Lebanon) in 1887.

4 Ishtar Gate
The Ishtar Gate, built by King Nebuchadnezzar II in 575 BC, was decorated with ceramic brick panels of dragons and bulls **(right)**. The Processional Way through the gate was lined with 120 lions.

5 Hattuşa Sphinx
This stone feline, dating from 13th century BC, was one of four discovered in the great Hittite city at Hattuşa (Boğazkale) in Anatolia.

2 Alexander Sarcophagus
Its high-relief frieze shows scenes of Alexander in battle against the Persians, but the Alexander Sarcophagus **(above)**, dating from the late 4th century BC, is in fact the tomb of King Abdalonymos of Sidon (died c.312 BC). Faint traces remain of the gaudy colour that would once have covered it.

3 Halikarnassos Lion
The tomb of King Mausolus was one of the seven wonders of the ancient world – this simple lion **(left)** is a surviving relic.

Key to floorplan
- Third floor
- Second floor
- First floor
- Ground floor

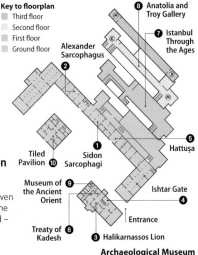

8 Anatolia and Troy Gallery
7 Istanbul Through the Ages
Alexander Sarcophagus 2
5 Hattuşa
1 Sidon Sarcophagi
Tiled Pavilion 10
Ishtar Gate 4
Museum of the Ancient Orient 9
Entrance
Treaty of Kadesh 6
3 Halikarnassos Lion

Archaeological Museum

6 Treaty of Kadesh

The world's oldest surviving peace treaty, carved in stone in 1269 BC, was agreed by Egyptian Pharaoh Ramses II and King Hattusili III of the Hittites after a battle in present-day Syria. It lays out the terms of the cease-fire and agrees the safe return of refugees.

ANCIENT WELCOME

Visitors are greeted by an eclectic assortment of archaeological artifacts. In the entrance hall to the main museum stands a statue of the Egyptian god Bes. At the foot of the stairs to the Museum of the Ancient Orient are two basalt lions from Samal, dating from the 8th century BC. Outside the main museum are porphyry sarcophagi, from the 4th–5th century AD, thought to be those of Byzantine emperors. The portico itself is modelled on the 4th-century-BC Sarcophagus of the Mourning Women.

9 Museum of the Ancient Orient

This museum **(right)** houses exhibits from Mesopotamia, Egypt and Babylon, including some of the world's first known writing – cuneiform clay tablets from 2700 BC.

10 Tiled Pavilion

Built in 1472 as a sports pavilion **(below)**, this is the oldest secular building in Istanbul. A masterpiece of İznik tiles itself, the pavilion also tells the interesting story of Turkish ceramics, with displays from İznik and Kutahya.

7 Istanbul Through the Ages

This thoughtful exhibit provides a fascinating insight into the city's history, with maps, plans and drawings alongside exhibits such as the original 14th-century bell from the Galata Tower.

8 Anatolia and Troy Gallery

Thousands of years of history are imaginatively timelined in this gallery through artifacts **(right)**. You can travel through Anatolia from the Stone Age to the Iron Age or follow the history of Troy from 3000 BC to the 1st century AD.

NEED TO KNOW

MAP S3 ■ Osman Hamdi Bey Yokuşu, Topkapı Sarayı, Gülhane ■ (0212) 520 77 40 ■ www.istanbularkeoloji.gov.tr

Open mid-Apr–Sep: 9am–7pm daily; Oct–mid-Apr: 9am–5pm daily

Adm ₺30

■ Due to ongoing construction, some rooms may be closed. Call ahead to check.

■ There is a small café on site and a good souvenir shop next to it.

TOP10 ★ Grand Bazaar

From the painted arches to the shopfronts gleaming with lanterns, piled with carpets or heaped with spices, the Grand Bazaar (Kapalı Çarşı) is a fantasy of Eastern opulence. Founded in 1461 by Sultan Mehmet II, the bazaar was designed as the trading heart of an empire. In addition to shops, banks, storerooms and cafés, it had mosques, travellers' accommodation, a bathhouse and a school. Destroyed several times by earthquake and fire, it has always bounced back. It offers a compelling and entertaining day out.

İç Bedesten ①
This was the bazaar's first building **(right)**, a Byzantine structure converted in 1461 into a sturdy lock-up in which jewellery was traded and slaves were auctioned. Today, it is used to sell precious goods such as antiques and rare icons.

② Jewellers' Street
(Kalpakçılar Caddesi)
The bazaar's widest street runs along the southern edge of the market, its shop windows piled high with jewels and precious metals. Some 100,000 kg (220,460 lb) of gold is traded in the bazaar each year. Gold jewellery **(right)** is sold by weight.

⑤ Street Names
At one time, each part of the bazaar had its own specialism, as indicated by the street names. Look for the slipper-makers *(terlikçiler)*, mirror-makers *(aynacılar)*, fez-makers *(fesçiler)*, quilt-makers *(yorgancılar)*, silk-thread-makers *(kazazcılar)* and fur-makers *(kürkçüler)*.

③ Carpet Sellers
The bazaar is home to Istanbul's finest carpet dealers **(above)** and lesser traders keen to sell you a hall runner or a bedside rug. Shops are scattered throughout the market, especially near the İç Bedesten on Halıcılar Caddesi.

④ Outdoor Stalls
Surrounding the covered market is a maze of tiny lanes, with stalls selling carpets, souvenirs, clothes and vegetables. Locals shop here.

⑥ Fountains
Two marble and copper fountains **(right)** provided drinking water for the market traders before modern plumbing was installed. An 1880 survey noted there were also 16 drinking-water posts, one fountain reservoir and eight wells for firefighters.

7 Sandal Bedesten

In the southeast corner of the bazaar, the 15th-century Sandal Bedesten is the second oldest part of the bazaar. The roof of its arcade consists of 20 brick domes propped up by pillars. It is the former antiques market.

8 Gates

Twenty-two gates lead into the covered bazaar from all directions **(right)**. The Beyazıt Gate, rebuilt after an earthquake in 1894, is marked with the *tuğra* (imperial sign) of Sultan Abdül Hamit II, and the assurance that "God loves tradesmen".

10 *200 metres (219 yards)*

Grand Bazaar

9 Zincirli Han

The *hans* provided accommodation, food and stables for travelling traders. This one, the oldest of 40 in the area, has been lovingly restored and is now occupied by Şişko Osman, a leading carpet dealer.

10 Valide Han

Located on Mahmutpaşa Yokuşu, this huge building, constructed in 1651, has been sadly neglected. Today, it contains a mix of residential, gallery and workshop space.

NEED TO KNOW

MAP N3 ▪ (0212) 519 12 48

Open 9am–7pm Mon–Sat (surrounding street markets are usually open longer and also on Sun)

▪ The bathhouse, school and hotels that were once part of the bazaar are long gone; now the market has a police station, ATM machines, public toilets and other necessities to keep its droves of visitors safe and happy.

▪ There are small tea and coffee shops scattered throughout the market, as well as several good kebab shops, a couple of restaurants and a range of upmarket cafés.

FACTS AND FIGURES

The Grand Bazaar is one of the world's largest buildings, containing a network of 61 covered streets and enclosing an area of 307,000 sq m (3,305,000 sq ft). Every day in this teeming marketplace, as many as 30,000 traders in 4,500 shops befriend and haggle with up to 400,000 shoppers – both locals and visitors from all around the world. In business since its foundation in 1461, the bazaar is the world's oldest covered market.

Following pages Vast nave of the Haghia Sophia

🔟 ⭐ Süleymaniye Mosque Complex

One of the finest creations of the Ottoman Empire's greatest architect, Sinan, Süleymaniye Camii was built in 1550–57 for Süleyman I. This hilltop mosque was constructed as part of a charitable foundation *(külliye)*. The mosque's dome and minarets dominate the skyline in a matchless display of imperial power, while its delicate calligraphy, stained-glass windows and decorative carvings add a lightness of touch. Süleyman and his wife Roxelana are buried in tombs in the courtyard.

Mosque Interior ①

The interior is simple and serene. The blue, white and gold dome **(right)** contains 200 stained-glass windows. The *mihrab* and pulpit are made from white marble with İznik tiles.

② Süleyman's Tomb

Sultan Süleyman I, "the Magnificent", lies in a grandiose garden tomb **(below)**, with an ebony, mother-of-pearl and ivory door and a dome inlaid with ceramic stars.

③ Sinan's Tomb

Sinan's mausoleum is on the site of the house he lived in when he was building the mosque, just beyond the northwest corner of the complex. It is a modest memorial to a prodigious talent.

④ Courtyard

This great courtyard **(below)** is surrounded by a colonnade of porphyry, Marmara and pink Egyptian columns, said to be recycled from the Hippodrome.

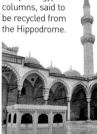

⑤ Hamam

The *hamam* in this mosque is a mixed-sex bathhouse, which makes it especially good for families. Sultan Süleyman was a frequent visitor to the bathhouse. Somewhat alarmingly, it offers all visitors free life insurance during their bath!

⑥ Caravanserai

The mosque was a full-service complex in the past – in the inn *(caravanserai)*, visitors could find food and lodging.

7 Medreses
Two of the six *medreses* (above), or colleges, – once part of the Imperial religious school providing theological and general education – house Süleyman's library of 110,000 manuscripts.

Süleymaniye Mosque Complex

NEED TO KNOW

MAP M2 ■ Prof Sıddık Sami Onar Cad ■ (0212) 522 02 98

Open 9am–7pm daily (closed at prayer times)

Süleyman's tomb: open 9:30am–4:30pm daily

Hamam: open 7am–midnight daily; adm; www.suleymaniye hamami.com.tr

....

■ Take some time out to admire the restored wooden houses in the nearby streets.

■ There are many refreshment options, with the Darüzziyafe Restaurant *(see p73)* in the old soup kitchen, the Lalezar Café *(Küçük Çamlıca Mahallesi)* and a row of cafés serving Turkish baked beans right opposite the main entrance to the complex.

8 İmaret
The mosque kitchens not only fed the many workers, students, teachers and priests in the complex (above), but ran a soup kitchen for up to 1,000 people a day.

9 Addicts' Alley
The cafés of "Addicts' Alley", formally known as Prof Sıddık Sami Onar Caddesi, once sold opium and hashish. It still has its cafés, but now the drug of choice is tobacco smoked in a water pipe *(nargile)*.

SINAN

Mimar Sinan, who built 146 mosques and 300 other buildings, never trained as an architect. Born into a Christian family in 1489, he was conscripted to serve in the sultan's Janissary Corps. He went on to become Commander of the Infantry Cadet Corps, responsible for military engineering, then in 1536 was made the Architect of the Abode of Felicity by the Sultan. He held the post until his death in 1588.

10 Views
The terraced gardens outside the main complex offer fine views (below) across the Golden Horn.

TOP 10 ⭐ Church of St Saviour in Chora

The Church of St Saviour in Chora is home to one of the world's finest collections of Byzantine art: more than 100 magnificent mosaics and frescoes depicting biblical images. They were commissioned in 1315–21 by Byzantine statesman Theodore Metochites, who also restored the 11th-century church on the site. The church was converted into a mosque in 1511 and is known by locals as Kariye Mosque (Kariye Camii). Its works of art slipped into obscurity until they were rediscovered in 1860.

Exterior ①
Walk round the back of the church **(right)** to experience the full impact of its architecture – masonry of striped marble, six domes, layers of arches, undulating rooflines and, to one side, a minaret.

② Genealogy of Christ
The two domes of the inner narthex (western entrance) portray 66 of Christ's forebears. In one dome **(above)**, the Virgin and Child survey the kings of the House of David. In the other, Christ is surrounded by ancestors including Adam, Abraham, Jacob and Jacob's 12 sons.

③ Anastasis Fresco
This resurrection fresco **(below)** depicts Christ pulling Adam and Eve from their graves, while the gates of hell are broken and Satan lies bound at Christ's feet.

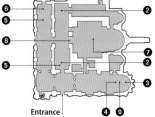

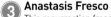

Church of St Saviour in Chora

④ Paracclesion
South of the church, the frescoes here depict judgment and resurrection. The unmarked tomb in the north wall may be of Theodore Metochites.

⑤ Ministry of Christ
The vaults of seven bays in the outer narthex and the south bay of the inner narthex detail the ministry of Christ, including his temptation and miracles such as healing of the sick.

8 Mosaic of Theodore Metochites

Over the door leading from the inner narthex to the nave is a superb mosaic **(left)** depicting Theodore Metochites in a large turban presenting his church to Christ, who raises a hand in blessing.

9 The Last Judgment

In the main dome of the Paracclesion is a vision of the Last Judgment, with Christ in Majesty flanked by the Virgin Mary, John the Baptist and the Apostles.

10 Life of the Virgin

Twenty mosaics **(right)** in the inner narthex depict the life of the Virgin Mary, based on the apocryphal 2nd-century Gospel of St James. They include images of Mary's first steps (at six months old).

CHURCH GUIDE

You now enter through a side door, but originally entry was by way of a long porch, the outer narthex, which leads into an inner narthex. The majority of the mosaics line the ceilings and walls of the twin narthexes. The inner narthex opens into the main body of the church (the nave). The altar is at the far end in front of the semicircular apse, flanked by the Prothesis (Communion chapel) and Diakonikon (vestry). On the south side is the Paracclesion (funerary chapel).

6 Infancy of Christ

Scenes from Christ's infancy are depicted in the semicircular panels of the outer narthex. Based on New Testament accounts, they include the Journey to Bethlehem, Mary and Joseph enrolling for taxation, the Nativity, and the terrible Massacre of the Innocents.

7 Dormition of the Virgin

This beautiful mosaic in the nave **(below)** shows Christ sitting beside his mother's coffin, cradling a baby that represents her soul. Above is Ashrael, the Angel of Death.

NEED TO KNOW

MAP B2 ■ Kariye Camii Sok, Kariye Meydanı, Edirnekapı ■ (0212) 631 92 41

Open mid-Apr–Sep: 9am–7pm daily; Oct– mid-Apr: 9am–5pm daily

Adm ₺45

■ Photography is permitted, but flash is forbidden.

■ The nave is often undergoing restoration so some artworks may not be accessible.

■ The Asitane Restaurant next door (see p79) is a garden restaurant, and one of the best places in the city for traditional Ottoman cuisine.

🔟 ⭐ Çemberlitaş Baths

No stay in Istanbul would be complete without a bout of steaming, soaping, scrubbing and massaging in a Turkish bath *(hamam)*. Çemberlitaş, built in 1584, is commonly hailed as one of the most beautiful. Designed by Sinan, it was commissioned by Selim II's wife, Nurbanu Sultan, as a way of providing financial support for the Atik Valide Sultan Mosque in Üsküdar, of which she was sponsor. Today, Çemberlitaş is still used by Turks, but is most popular with tourists and photographers – it's a regular location for film and fashion shoots.

1 Entrance
At the ticket office, you are given a *peştemal* **(below)**, which is a type of sarong, for modesty, a *kese*, a coarse mitt for scrubbing the body down, and tokens to give to the attendants. Men and women are then sent off to separate sections.

2 Men's Section
Originally the *hamam* consisted of two identical suites of rooms, each with a separate entrance. The men's section of the baths is still exactly as envisaged by its creator, Sinan.

3 Women's Section
The women's changing area was lost in 1868, when Divanyolu Caddesi was widened, so women now change in a corridor; but their hot room is unaltered.

5 Hot Room (Sıcaklık)
The hot room has a domed ceiling supported by 12 arches that rise from marble columns **(above)**. The dome is pitted with glass "elephants' eyes", which channel the light through the steam to polka-dot the floor.

4 Dressing Room
(Camekan)
In the dressing room **(above)**, an attendant will assign you a locker and give you a pair of slippers. Most people go nude under the *peştemal*, but wear a swimsuit if you wish to.

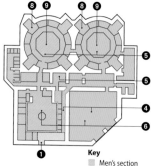

Çemberlitaş Baths

Key
■ Men's section
■ Women's section

ANCIENT CUSTOMS

The direct descendant of the Graeco-Roman bath, the *hamam* was eagerly adopted by Islamic invaders who really did believe that cleanliness is next to godliness. The bath became a chance not only to cleanse the skin and detoxify the body, but also to restore the spirit. For women, time in the *hamam* was a welcome escape from the narrow world in which they spent their daily lives, as well as a place for them to find potential daughters-in-law.

6 Cool Room (Soğukluk)

The cool room is the place to sit and chat. The men's is as elegant as it was in Sinan's day; the women's is more modern. Afterwards, head back to change, or go for your oil massage.

7 Oil Massage Room

You will be one of several people being massaged **(below)** on a row of beds under bright lights. It's worth any discomfort you may experience – you'll feel great afterwards.

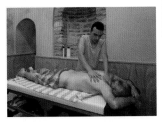

8 Private Cubicles (Halvets)

Around the walls are a number of private cubicles with taps running cold, warm and hot water, which you can use to wash or cool down if the heat gets too much for you.

9 Navel Stone (Göbek Taşı)

In the centre of the hot room is a large slab of marble. Lie down and wait for the attendant. You will be covered in soap suds, and scrubbed all over with the *kese*. Then you will be lathered again, washed with a cloth, and soap-massaged **(below)**. Finally, your hair will be washed, and you will be vigorously rinsed with buckets of water.

NEED TO KNOW

MAP P4 ▪ Vezir Hanı Cad 8 ▪ (0212) 522 79 74 ▪ www.cemberlitashamami.com

Open 6am–midnight daily

Adm ₺140 (₺220 with massage, ₺355 with oil massage)

▪ If you are planning to stay in the *hamam* for any length of time, take a small bottle of water in with you.

▪ The baths are situated halfway between the Sultanahmet Square and the Grand Bazaar, and are an easy walk from either. The surrounding area is bursting with cafés, teashops and restaurants – take your pick.

10 Extras

Take as much time as you like to return to the steam room or sit in the cool room. If you want the full works, the attendants will be happy to give you a manicure, pedicure or facial.

TOP 10 ⭐ Dolmabahçe Palace

In 1843, Sultan Abdül Mecit, who wanted to reinvent the Ottoman Empire in a European image, employed Armenian architects Garabet and Nikoğos Balyan to build a luxurious new palace on the Bosphorus shore. Dolmabahçe Sarayı, completed in 1856, is the result. Luxurious it certainly is, with 285 rooms and 43 reception halls, and lavish decoration in gold and crystal that rivals the Palace of Versailles in France. Ironically, this extravagance hastened the end of the Empire, and the last sultan fled from here into exile in 1922.

Ceremonial Hall ①
(Muayede Salonu)
The dome in this vast hall **(right)** is 36 m (118 ft) high. The Bohemian crystal chandelier, a gift from Queen Victoria of England, has 750 lights and weighs 4.5 tonnes (9,900 lb). It is the world's largest chandelier.

② Gates
The palace had two ceremonial entrances, both highly ornamented: the Treasury Gate, which is now the main entrance, and the Imperial Gate **(above)**. Both gates still have a guard of honour.

③ Waterfront Façade
The marble façade **(below)** is 284 m (930 ft) long. The State Rooms are on the left, the Ceremonial Hall in the centre and the Harem on the right.

④ Harem
The apartments in the Harem are furnished to various grades of luxury (for the sultan, his mother, wives, concubines, servants and guests) – also baths, a school, a maternity ward and a central salon where the concubines and wives would meet for tea.

⑤ State Rooms (Selamlık)
The rooms on the palace's seaward side were used by the Grand Vizier and ministers, while those on the landward side were administrative offices. They are all lavishly decorated.

⑥ Sultan's Bathrooms
The Sultan had two bathrooms: one in the main palace, faced in marble; the other in the Harem, decorated in violet flowers.

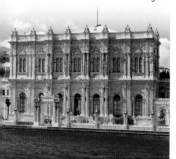

7 Crystal Staircase

The ornate staircase **(above)** has balusters of Baccarat crystal. It links the administrative offices with the ceremonial rooms upstairs.

ATATÜRK

Born in 1881, Mustafa Kemal rose to prominence in 1915, leading Turkish forces to victory at Gallipoli. A leader of the Young Turks republican movement, he seized his moment following the end of World War I, abolishing the sultanate in 1922 and declaring a republic in 1923. As Turkey's first president, he westernized the country – introducing the Latin alphabet, compulsory schooling and rights for women. He is still idolized as the "Father of the Turks" (Atatürk); it is illegal in Turkey to criticize him publicly.

10 Atatürk's Rooms

In the first years of the republic, Atatürk used the palace as his Istanbul base, keeping an office and bedroom **(below)** in the Harem. He died here, from cirrhosis of the liver, on 10 November 1938 – all the palace's clocks are set to 9:05am, the moment of his death.

8 Clock Tower

The four-storey tower, 27 m (90 ft) high, was added to the palace in 1890, during the reign of Sultan Abdül Hamit II *(see p91)*. The clock – which still keeps time – was built by the celebrated Parisian clock-maker Paul Garnier.

9 Gardens

The palace and gardens **(below)** stand on reclaimed land (the name Dolmabahçe means "Filled Garden"). In addition to the palace and its 16 external pavilions, the grounds once held a flour mill, pharmacy, aviary, glass factory and foundry.

NEED TO KNOW

MAP C5 ■ Dolmabahçe Cad ■ (0212) 236 90 00 ■ Tram: Kabataş, then a 5-minute walk ■ www. millisaraylar.gov.tr

Open 9am–4pm Tue–Sun

Adm ₺60 for Selamlık, ₺40 for Harem

■ Admission to the palace is through guided tour only. There are two different itineraries: one of the Selamlık (areas reserved for men, including the Ceremonial Hall); the other of the Harem (including the living quarters of the royal women, the sultan's private quarters, and Atatürk's bedroom, bathroom and study).

■ There is a café in the Clock Tower, and toilets near both entrances.

🔟 ⭐ Bosphorus Cruise

The Istanbul skyline is justifiably one of the most famous cityscapes in the world and, while there are many places from which to admire it, by far the best is the deck of a boat on the Bosphorus. After the bustle of the city centre, a trip up the Bosphorus gives you an entirely different perspective on the city. Give your lungs a break from the traffic fumes and your feet a rest from trudging pavements. Take the local ferry for a modest fare, and spend a day floating serenely along the straits past magnificent shores and wooden villas.

1 Eminönü Pier
The Bosphorus ferry departs from Eminönü port **(above)**, the city's busiest ferry terminal. Pick up a *simit* or fish sandwich from a street vendor.

2 Leander's Tower
(Kız Kulesi)
This tower *(see p97)*, off the Üsküdar shore, is a restaurant. Its Turkish name means "Maiden's Tower", after a legendary princess kept there; the English name refers to a hero of Greek myth.

3 Dolmabahçe Palace
(Dolmabahçe Sarayı)
Sultan Abdül Mecit virtually mortgaged the Ottoman Empire to build this lavish, European-style palace in the 1850s.

4 Ortaköy
One of the prettiest villages on the straits, at the foot of the Bosphorus Bridge, Ortaköy **(below)** is a weekend retreat for İstanbulites.

5 Bosphorus Bridge
(Boğaziçi Köprüsü)
Completed in 1973, this bridge is 1,510 m (4,954 ft) long and stretches between Ortaköy and Beylerbeyi. It was the first to link Europe and Asia.

IT'S ALL A MYTH

When Greek goddess Hera sent a swarm of gnats to plague Io, her rival for the affections of the god Zeus, Io turned herself into a cow and swam across the straits to escape, giving the Bosphorus its name – the "Ford of the Cow". In another Greek myth, Jason and the Argonauts rowed up the Bosphorus in search of the Golden Fleece – perhaps an echo of the Black Sea tradition of using a lamb's fleece to trap gold when panning.

Bosphorus Cruise

6 Beylerbeyi Palace (Asian Side)
(Beylerbeyi Sarayı)

This palace **(above)** was built as a summer annexe to the Dolmabahçe. It had no kitchens, and food was rowed across as required.

9 Sarıyer

This village is the main fishing port on the Bosphorus. It has a historic fish market, as well as several good fish restaurants near the shore.

10 Anadolu Kavağı (Asian Side)

This is the last stop **(below)** for the ferry, and the locals make a good living selling fish lunches and ice cream to tourists. The 14th-century Yoros Kalesi, a Genoese Castle, affords good views.

7 Arnavutköy and Bebek

The pretty 19th-century wooden villas (yalıs) that line the waterfront along this central stretch of the Bosphorus are some of the city's most desirable real estate.

8 Fortress of Europe
(Rumeli Hisarı)

This castle **(below)** was built by Mehmet the Conqueror in 1452 prior to his attack on Constantinople. Across the water stands the Fortress of Asia (Anadolu Hisarı), built in the late 14th century.

NEED TO KNOW

MAP F4 ▪ Departs from Eminönü Boğaz Hattı Pier ▪ (0212) 444 18 51 ▪ en.sehirhatlari.istanbul/en

Long cruise: May–Oct: 1:35pm daily, Nov–Apr: 10:35am daily; fare ₺15 one way, ₺25 return

Short cruise: 2:30pm daily; fare ₺12

▪ The return cruise takes about 6 hours. If you wish to visit sights en route, take the ferry one way and return by bus. The bus, however, can be very slow.

▪ Food is available on the ferry and there are various food facilities at the last stop in Anadolu Kavağı.

▪ A 2-hour round-trip cruise runs from Eminönü to the Bosphorus Bridge.

The Top 10
of Everything

Basilica Cistern, an underground water
reservoir constructed in the 6th century

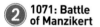 Moments in History

① AD 330–95: Division of the Roman Empire

In 330, Constantine moved the capital of the Empire from Rome to the former Greek colony of Byzantium. It was initially called New Rome but later became Constantinople ("City of Constantine"). In 395, Theodosius divided the Empire between his sons, with the western half run from Rome and the eastern (Byzantine) half centred on Constantinople.

Bust of Constantine

② 1071: Battle of Manzikert

The Seljuk Turks coming from Persia defeated Byzantine forces at Manzikert and seized most of Anatolia. The Byzantines never recovered their eastern lands.

③ 1204: Sack and Capture of Constantinople

The armies of the Fourth Crusade sacked Constantinople, driving the emperor into exile. Crusader rulers governed in Constantinople until 1261, when Byzantine Emperor Michael VIII Palaeologus recaptured the city.

Capture of Constantinople in 1204

④ 1453: Conquest of Constantinople

Following years of Ottoman encroachment into the Byzantine Empire, Sultan Mehmet II captured Constantinople, converting the church of Haghia Sophia into the mosque of Ayasofya. The last Byzantine emperor, Constantine XI, died fighting on the city walls.

⑤ 1529: Siege of Vienna

The Ottoman Empire reached its maximum extent under Süleyman I *(see p62)*. By 1526 he had control of southern Hungary. In the spring of 1529, he mustered a huge military force with the aim of consolidating his Hungarian gains and moving on to Vienna. A combination of serious flooding en route and a spirited defence led by a German mercenary, Niklas Graf Salm, sent the Turks packing and marked the end of Ottoman expansion in Western Europe.

⑥ 1777: Turkish Delight

Ali Muhiddin Hacı Bekir, confectioner to the imperial court, invented a chewy sweet flavoured with rosewater and coated in icing sugar: *rahat lokum* ("morsel of contentment"), better known as Turkish delight.

⑦ 1853–6: Crimean War

When Russia began to encroach on Ottoman territory, Britain and France weighed in on the side of the Turks. Englishwoman Florence Nightingale *(see p97)* set up a hospital in Istanbul, defining modern nursing practice.

Atatürk Mustafa Kemal

8 1919–23: Birth of the Republic

Mustafa Kemal – or Atatürk ("Father of the Turks") – led a bloodless revolution that abolished the sultanate, and fought a fierce war of independence. In 1923, as first president of the new Republic of Turkey, he moved the capital to Ankara, leaving Istanbul without political status for the first time in 1,600 years.

Construction of the Bosphorus Bridge

9 1973: Bosphorus Bridge

The Bosphorus Bridge was opened between Ortaköy and Beylerbeyi, linking European Turkey to Asian Anatolia.

10 2018: AKP win Fifth Term

The June 2018 elections saw the Justice and Development Party (AKP) win a fifth term in government, resulting in increased powers for its leader, and Turkish president, Recep Tayyip Erdoğan.

TOP 10 NOTABLE OTTOMAN SULTANS

1 Osman Gazi (1299–1326)
The Ottoman dynasty takes its name from that of its founder, Osman. In 1301, his forces won the first Ottoman victory against the Byzantine Empire at the Battle of Baphaeon.

2 Orhan Gazi (1326–60)
Orhan moved the Ottoman capital to Bursa and established Islam as the state religion.

3 Murat I (1360–89)
Murat founded the Janissary Corps, an elite group within the Ottoman army.

4 Mehmet II the Conqueror (1451–81)
In 1453, Mehmet captured Constantinople from its Byzantine rulers. He laid out a new city on the rubble, and founded Topkapı Palace.

5 Süleyman I the Magnificent (1520–66)
A conqueror, lawmaker and patron of the arts, Süleyman presided over the golden age of Ottoman rule (see p62).

6 Mehmet III (1595–1603)
Mehmet's mother had 18 of his 19 brothers strangled so that he could take the throne.

7 Osman II (1618–22)
The Janissaries killed Osman at Yedikule after his failed attempt to curb their power.

8 Mahmut II (1808–39)
Mahmut wiped out the Janissary Corps, slaughtering thousands in the purge.

9 Abdül Hamit II (1876–1909)
Abdül Hamit built Yıldız Sarayı, the last of the imperial palaces.

10 Mehmet VI (1918–22)
The last of the Ottoman sultans fled into European exile in November 1922.

Sultan Mehmet II

🔟 Places of Worship

Süleymaniye Mosque Complex

1 Süleymaniye Mosque Complex
(Süleymaniye Camii)

This vast mosque (see pp26–7), which dominates the skyline of the Golden Horn, is the crowning achievement of Koca Mimar Sinan, greatest of imperial architects. Built in 1550–57 in the grounds of the old palace, Eski Saray, it is a suitably grand memorial to its founder, Süleyman I (see p62).

2 Blue Mosque
(Sultanahmet Camii)

Commissioned by Sultan Ahmet I, the magnificent Blue Mosque (see pp18–19) was built by the imperial architect Sedefkar Mehmet Ağa, a pupil of the great Sinan, in 1609–16. The mosque takes its name from the blue İznik tiles that line its inner walls.

3 Fatih Mosque
(Fatih Camii)

The original Fatih Mosque was built by Mehmet II to celebrate his capture of Constantinople in 1453; its name means "the Conqueror's mosque". The present mosque (see p75) was built in the 18th century by Mustafa III, after an earthquake in 1766 destroyed the original.

Detail, Fatih Mosque

4 Eyüp Sultan Mosque
(Eyüp Camii)

Also rebuilt after the 1766 earthquake, this mosque (see p76) at the top of the Golden Horn is one of the holiest places in Islam. It is built around the tomb of a 7th-century saint, Eyüp el-Ensari, standard-bearer of the Prophet Mohammed.

5 Atik Valide Mosque
(Atik Valide Camii)

One of Istanbul's finest mosques (see p100) and Sinan's last great work, the "Old Mosque of the Sultan's Mother" was completed in 1583 for the formidable Nurbanu, wife of Selim III and mother of Murat III.

Interior of the Atik Valide Mosque

6 Church of St George
(Ortodoks Patrikhanesi)

The Church of St George (see p78) stands within the Greek Orthodox Patriarchate complex. Built in 1720, it includes a superb 11th-century mosaic of the Virgin Mary.

7 Armenian Patriarchate
(Ermeni Patrikhanesi)

MAP M6 ■ Sevgi Sok 6, Kumkapı

The Armenians came in numbers

to Istanbul in 1461, invited by Sultan Mehmet the Conqueror to help rebuild the city after its capture in 1453. Opposite the patriarchate building, the Church of the Holy Mother of God (Surp Asdvadzadzin) serves as the main church for the now sadly dwindling Armenian community.

8 Church of St Mary of the Mongols (Kanlı Kilise)

Princess Maria, illegitimate daughter of Byzantine Emperor Michael VIII Palaeologos, married Khan Abaqa of the Mongols. On his death in 1282, she founded a convent and this church – Istanbul's only Greek Orthodox church to have been granted immunity from conversion to a mosque by Mehmet the Conqueror.

9 Christ Church

Consecrated in 1868 as the Crimean Memorial Church, this fine Gothic Revival building *(see p86)* was renovated and renamed in the 1990s. It is the largest Protestant church in Istanbul.

10 Church of St Anthony of Padua (Sent Antuan Kilisesi)

The Church of St Anthony of Padua *(see p86)* is Istanbul's largest Roman Catholic church. Built in 1906–12, it is home to a small community of Franciscan monks.

The Church of St Anthony of Padua

TOP 10 TIPS ON ISLAMIC ETIQUETTE

Women near Haghia Sophia

1 Covering the Head
It is essential for women to cover their heads when entering a mosque.

2 Dress
Dress modestly – no bare knees, shoulders or midriffs (for either sex).

3 Shoes
You must remove your shoes before entering a mosque or a Turkish home.

4 Men and Women
A man should not touch a woman (other than family), even to shake hands, unless the woman proffers her hand or cheek first.

5 Sightseeing
Don't go sightseeing in mosques at prayer times (particularly around midday on Fridays).

6 Joking about Islam
Don't joke about Islam or criticize anything related to it.

7 Left Hand
In some Islamic countries one should avoid eating or passing food with the left hand; in Turkey this is not observed.

8 Pork and Alcohol
Although many people in Turkey do drink alcohol, you should never offer alcohol or pork to a Muslim – and do not consume any yourself if unsure of your companions' views.

9 Family Rooms
Some restaurants and cafés have separate family rooms *(aile salonu)* into which women will automatically be conducted. Men may only sit there with their families.

10 Ramazan (Ramadan)
Avoid eating and drinking in public during daylight hours in the month-long fast of Ramazan.

TOP 10 Byzantine Monuments

Haghia Sophia as seen from Sultanahmet Square

1 Haghia Sophia (Ayasofya)
Built by Emperor Justinian in the 6th century, Haghia Sophia *(see pp16–17)* is one of the world's greatest architectural achievements. Justinian was so proud of his basilica that he proclaimed: "Glory to God who has thought me worthy to finish this work. Solomon, I have outdone you".

2 Hippodrome (At Meydanı)
Once a Byzantine race track 450 m (1,500 ft) long, the Hippodrome *(see p60)* could hold 100,000 people. It was the scene of celebrations and, on occasion, bloodshed; the Nika Riots in 532 ended with 30,000 dead.

3 Cisterns
To ensure good water supply in times both of peace and of siege, the Byzantines built a series of vast underground water cisterns beneath their city. The finest are the Basilica Cistern *(see p63)* and the Cistern of 1,001 Columns *(see p64)*.

The underground Basilica Cistern

4 Church of St Saviour in Chora (Kariye Camii)
The main reason to visit this 11th-century Byzantine church *(see pp28–9)* is its glorious collection of mosaics and frescoes, which depict biblical scenes.

Section of the Theodosian Walls

5 Theodosian Walls
(Teodos II Surları)
MAP A5
Over the course of 1,000 years, the curtain walls *(see p54)* built by Emperor Theodosius II in 412–22 proved to be a necessity – they withstood more than 20 attacks by Huns, Arabs, Bulgarians, Turks and Russians, finally succumbing to the Ottomans in 1453 *(see p38)*. The walls have now been partially restored.

6 Great Palace Mosaic Museum
(Büyük Saray Mozaikleri Müzesi)
Only fragments remain of the Great Palace of the Byzantine emperors. This small museum *(see p64)* houses

one of them – the mosaic passageway, discovered in the 1930s, that led from the palace to the royal box in the Hippodrome. The floor depicts wild animals and hunting scenes.

7 Church of SS Sergius and Bacchus
(Küçük Ayasofya Camii)
In the historic heart of the city, just south of Sultanahmet Square, the Church of SS Sergius and Bacchus *(see p65)* was built in the 6th century and has an original Greek frieze.

8 Aqueduct of Valens
(Bozdoğan Kemeri)
This beautifully preserved 4th-century aqueduct *(see p75)*, which remained in use until the 19th century, was a key part of the system that carried fresh water into the Byzantine capital from the forests of Thrace.

9 Haghia Eirene
(Aya İrini Kilisesi)
One of the oldest churches in the city, Haghia Eirene *(see p65)* stands in the outer courtyard of the Topkapı Palace. The church was rebuilt in the 6th century and acted as a sister church to the nearby Haghia Sophia. Today the church is open to the public and, because of its excellent acoustics, concerts are often held here.

10 Church of the Pammakaristos
(Fethiye Camii)
This 12th-century Byzantine church *(see p75)* served as the worldwide headquarters of the Greek Orthodox faith during the 15th and 16th centuries. It was converted to a mosque in 1573. The former funerary chapel now functions as a museum housing magnificent mosaics.

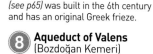

Mosaic, Church of the Pammakaristos

TOP 10 NOTABLE BYZANTINE RULERS

Sovereign Theodora and Antonina

1 Constantine (306–37)
Constantine moved the capital of the Roman Empire from Rome to Constantinople in 330 AD *(see p38)*.

2 Theodosius II (408–50)
Emperor Theodosius codified the law, founded a university and built the city walls *(see p77)*.

3 Justinian I (527–65)
Justinian founded many great buildings, including Haghia Sophia *(see pp16–17)*, as well as reforming the law.

4 Theodora (527–48)
A bear-keeper's daughter turned stripper and prostitute, Theodora ruled alongside her husband Justinian I.

5 Justinian II (685–95 and 705–11)
Justinian's enemies deposed him then cut off his nose, because a disfigured man could not be emperor. He later regained the throne wearing, it is said, a prosthetic nose of solid gold.

6 Irene of Athens (797–802)
Irene was the first woman to rule the Empire on her own.

7 Basil I (867–86)
The homosexual lover of Michael III, Basil was crowned joint emperor in 866, then killed Michael to rule alone.

8 Zoë (1028–50)
Zoë wed three times after becoming empress aged 50.

9 Romanus IV Diogenes (1067–71)
Romanus was defeated by the Seljuks at Manzikert in 1071 and as a result he was exiled.

10 Constantine XI Palaeologus (1449–53)
The last of the Byzantines died fighting on the city walls during the conquest of 1453.

Museums and Galleries

Bright exterior of the Istanbul Modern at night

1 Istanbul Modern

For centuries, Turkish art was better known for tradition rather than innovation, but contemporary Turkish artists are exploring new avenues. Set in a beautifully converted Bosphorus warehouse, Istanbul Modern *(see p91)* is an ideal platform for showcasing art from the 19th to the 21st centuries.

2 Topkapı Palace
(Topkapı Sarayı)

The buildings here *(see pp12–15)* are spectacular, and some of the collections are even more so – from the sea of Chinese porcelain in the kitchens to the Treasury, with its display of jewellery, carved ivory and great rocks of emerald. Religious treasures include hair from the Prophet's beard.

Ceramic pot at the Pera Museum in Beyoğlu

3 Archaeological Museum
(Arkeoloji Müzesi)

Don't miss the marble tomb of Abdalonymus of Sidon, known as the "Alexander Sarcophagus" *(see pp20–21)*. It depicts Alexander the Great defeating the Persians at the Battle of Issus in 333 BC.

4 Military Museum
(Askeri Müze)

Among the many fascinating exhibits at this museum *(see p84)* are *cembiyes* (curved daggers) carried by 15th-century Ottoman foot soldiers, and the vast imperial tents used by sultans during their military campaigns. The Mehter Band, founded in the 14th century, plays Ottoman military music daily at 3pm.

5 Pera Museum
(Pera Müzesi)

The Pera *(see p85)* is a privately run museum with an intriguing mix of fine art, such as Vanmour's *Women Drinking Coffee (see p15)*, modern exhibitions and ancient weights and measures.

6 Sakıp Sabancı Museum
(Sakıp Sabancı Müzesi)

Known locally as the "Horse Mansion", this museum *(see p93)* houses the collection of the late Turkish business tycoon Sakıp Sabancı. The displays encompass 500 years of Ottoman calligraphy, and Ottoman and Turkish painting of the 19th and 20th centuries. Major touring art exhibitions are also hosted here.

7 Museum of Turkish and Islamic Arts
(Türk ve İslam Eserleri Müzesi)

This wonderful collection, in the 16th-century palace *(see p61)* of İbrahim Paşa, spans 1,300 years of the finest works of Turkish and Islamic art. Among the exhibits are splendid Turkish carpets, calligraphy and ethnographic items.

8 Rahmi Koç Museum
(Rahmi Koç Müzesi)

An Ottoman foundry and nearby shipyard on the Golden Horn are the perfect setting for this world-class collection *(see pp76–7)* of all things mechanical, from vintage cars to model planes – and even a submarine.

9 Sadberk Hanım Museum (Sadberk Hanım Müzesi)

Two lovingly restored Bosphorus mansions house an inspiring collection *(see p93)* of ancient Anatolian artifacts, Ottoman costumes and ceramics.

Boats on display, Naval Museum

10 Naval Museum
(Deniz Müzesi)

For centuries, the Ottoman navy ruled the seas, and its achievements are celebrated here *(see p91)*. This marvellous museum was originally established in 1897. Among the exhibits are figureheads and engravings, but the flamboyantly decorated royal barges, which include the caïques and galleys, are the highlights of any visit.

Exhibits at SALT Beyoğlu

1 SALT Beyoğlu
Gallery complex housed in a beautifully restored 19th century apartment block on busy İstiklal Caddesi *(see p54)*.

2 Mevlevi Monastery
Whirling dervishes are the main draw in this monastery-turned-museum *(see p84)*.

3 Ottoman Bank Museum
MAP F3 ▪ Bankalar Cad 11, Galata ▪ (0212) 334 22 00
Delve into the intriguing vaults of a bank designed by Vallaury in 1890.

4 Railway Museum, Sirkeci Station
The *Orient Express* silver service is the star among 300 exhibits *(see p62)*.

5 SAV Automobile Museum
Inspect some of the best motor transport from the last century, from Rolls-Royce to Ferrari *(see p94)*.

6 Aşiyan Museum
A Bosphorus mansion pays homage to 20th-century poets and thinkers *(see p92)*.

7 Museum of the History of Science and Technology in Islam
MAP G4 ▪ Has Ahirlar Binası, Gülhane Parkı ▪ (0212) 528 80 65
See displays of historical tools from astronomy and medicine, to war.

8 Florence Nightingale Museum
The museum includes the nurse's private quarters and surgery room used during the Crimean War *(see p97)*.

9 Arter Gallery
MAP J5 ▪ İstiklal Cad 211 ▪ (0212) 243 37 67
The gallery hosts temporary exhibitions by internationally acclaimed artists.

10 Atatürk Museum
MAP T3 ▪ Halaskargazi Cad, Şişli ▪ (0212) 240 63 19
This suburban house is now a memorial museum to the great man.

🔟 Off the Beaten Track

1 Column of Marcian (Kıztaşı)

MAP C4 ■ Junction of Kıztaşı Cad with Dolap Sokak, Aksaray

Shorter in height but more impressive than the better-known Çemberlitaş (Column of Constantine), this granite column dates from the 5th century and has an ornate Corinthian capital with eagles, as well as a plinth carved with Nike, the goddess of victory.

Column of Marcian

2 Jewish Museum

MAP F2 ■ Neve Shalom Synagogue, Büyük Hendek Cad 61, Karaköy ■ (0212) 292 63 33 ■ Open 10am–4pm Mon–Thu, 10am–1pm Fri, 10am–2pm Sun ■ Adm ■ www.muze500.com

This interesting little museum is housed in the Nev Shalom syna-gogue, near the Galata Tower. The museum tells the story of the Jews who were offered sanctuary in Istanbul following their expulsion from Spain in the late 15th century.

3 Zoodochus Pege (Balıklı Kilise)

MAP A6 ■ Seyit Nizam Cad 3, Silivrikapı ■ (0212) 582 30 81 ■ Open 8:30am–4:30pm daily

This beautiful 19th-century Greek Orthodox church is set in lush green Christian and Muslim cemeteries. In a basement shrine, holy carp swim gracefully in the crystal-clear spring waters.

4 Depo

MAP G2 ■ Koltukçular Çıkmaz, Beyoğlu ■ (0212) 292 39 56 ■ Open 11am–7pm Tue–Sun ■ www.depoistanbul.net

Housed in a former tobacco warehouse, this hip but socially conscious gallery has an ever-changing series of exhibitions. Many of the shows focus on more offbeat subjects, such as the plight of Turkey's Christian minorities, political protests and the like. There are also regular documentary screenings.

5 Safa Meyhanesi

MAP A6 ■ İlyasbey Cad 121, Yedikule ■ (0212) 585 55 94

Arguably the city's most atmospheric *meyhane* (tavern), located in the

historic Yedikule quarter, a short stroll from the fortress of the same name. The decor hasn't changed since the 1940s, with vintage *rakı* (aniseed spirit) posters adorning the walls, high ceilings and wooden floors. Drink *rakı*, eat *meze* and fish and be merry.

6 Mihrimah Mosque
(Mihrimah Cami)

MAP J3 ■ Sulukule Cad, Edirnekapı ■ Open dawn–dusk daily

A masterpiece of the Ottoman architect Sinan and dedicated to the beautiful Mihrimah, daughter of Sultan Süleyman the Magnificent, this delightful mosque stands dramatically atop the Old City's highest hill. Its elegant interior is flooded with light from attractive stained-glass windows.

Ornate dome, Mihrimah Mosque

7 Vefa Bozacısı

MAP E4 ■ Vefa Cad 66, Fatih ■ 0212 519 49 22 ■ www.vefa.com.tr ■ Open 7am–midnight daily

Even if you don't fancy drinking the fermented millet drink (*boza*) for which this charming place is known, it's worth visiting for the late-19th-century interior, with its cut glass, dark wood and blue-and-white İznik tiles. The *boza* is made in the back.

8 Istanbul Municipality Building

MAP D4 ■ Sehzadebaşı Cad, Fatih ■ (0212) 512 55 00

Built in 1953, this huge, rectangular building's grid-like façade brought international, modern architecture into the heart of the Old City, apposite when you consider that Le Corbusier was influenced by Ottoman architecture following a visit to the city in 1911.

9 Edirnekapı Pigeon Fanciers' Market
(Güvercin Pazarı)

MAP J1

Every Saturday and Sunday, pigeon fanciers from across the city come to buy and sell tumbling pigeons at this fascinating bazaar in the shadow of the Byzantine Palace of the Porphyrogenitus (*see p78*). Drink a refreshing glass of tea with the old-timers in the teahouse opposite and soak up the atmosphere.

10 Emirgan Park

Istanbul's most beautiful park (*see p94*) is located by the Bosphorus, just above the second suspension bridge. Dotted with kösks, little wooden pavilions resembling Swiss chalets, it has a small lake and some children's play equipment. The park is awash with blooms during April's Tulip Festival (*see p56*) and provides a pleasant retreat from the city.

Resplendent Emirgan Park during the Tulip Festival

TOP10 Culinary Highlights

1 Meze

Most Turkish meals begin with *meze* – collections of small starters. The range of *meze* is vast, and you can easily eat enough for a whole meal. Cold options range from *haydari* (yogurt with mint and garlic) to *midye pilakisi* (mussels cooked in olive oil) or *çerkez tavuğu* (cold chicken in walnut and bread sauce). Hot options may include chicken liver kebabs, calamari, grilled cheese, or something more adventurous such as *koç yumurtası* (fried sheep's testicles).

2 İmam Bayıldı
("The Imam Fainted")

This strangely named dish of aubergine stuffed with tomatoes and onions is a Turkish classic – the Imam in question supposedly found it so delicious that he passed out in ecstasy. Aubergine is a fundamental ingredient of Turkish cuisine; it is said that Ottoman court chefs could prepare it in 150 ways.

İmam Bayıldı

3 Dolma

The word *dolma* means "filled up", and is used to describe any stuffed food, from walnuts to peppers, beef tomatoes or aubergine. The most common version, eaten cold, is vine leaves stuffed with rice, onion, nuts and herbs.

4 Kebabs and Köfte

Turkey's most famous culinary export is the kebab – called *kebap* in Turkish. *Döner kebap* is wafer-thin slices of roast meat (usually lamb) carved from a spit; the *şiş kebap* is cubed lamb or chicken grilled on a skewer. *Köfte* is minced meat cooked as meatballs or flattened onto a skewer and grilled as an *izgara kebap*.

5 Çoban Salatası
("Shepherd's Salad")

This salad combines tomato, cucumber, chopped pepper, lettuce, coriander, celery, lemon juice and olive oil in a light, healthy, colourful and refreshing dish. Turkish tomatoes are among the finest in the world.

6 Seafood

Istanbul's proximity to the sea means that *taze balık* (fresh fish) is very popular with locals. The catch of the day is often grilled and served with rice or chips and salad. Shellfish and calamari are served as *meze*. A delicious Black Sea dish is *hamsi pilavı* (fresh anchovies and rice).

Stuffed vine leaves or *dolma*

7 Stews (Güveç)

Often served in traditional *lokanta* restaurants *(see p110)* and generally popular in winter, hearty stews are mostly made with lamb, tomatoes and onions.

8 Börek

These savoury pastries are served either as part of a *meze* tray or on their own as fast food. They can be flat or rolled, and are filled with cheese and parsley, spinach or meat. They make an excellent light snack.

Turkish pastries on display

9 Pastries

Sweet pastries are sold in dedicated shops and by street vendors; tourist restaurants will offer them as dessert. The most famous is *baklava* (flaky pastry drenched in syrup), but there are many variations with honey, syrups, marzipan, almonds and pistachios. All are heavenly to eat.

10 Tea and Coffee

The lifeblood of Turkey, both *çay* (tea) and *kahve* (coffee) are drunk black, strong and sweet, in small quantities. Tea is served all day and on all occasions. You can ask for it weaker *(açık)* and without sugar. Coffee is drunk less frequently; it is more expensive than tea, and is served with a glass of water. All instant coffee is known as Nescafé.

Traditional black tea with lemon

TOP 10 CULINARY SPECIALITIES

Sliced *Gözleme* with cheese

1 *Gözleme*
A *gözleme* is a large rolled pancake with a savoury stuffing.

2 *İşkembe Çorbası*
Tripe soup is a local delicacy and is said to be very good for hangovers.

3 *Kanlıca* Yoghurt
Firm and creamy, the yogurt from Kanlıca is the country's finest.

4 *Lokum*
Turkish delight was invented by an Istanbul sweetmaker *(see p38)*. It's now available everywhere and in multiple flavours. The original shop *(Map Q2; Hamidiye Cad 81, Bahçekapı; (0212) 522 85 43)* is still open in its original location.

5 *Simit*
A *simit* is a round sesame bread, which is quite similar to a New York pretzel.

6 Elastic Ice Cream
Maraş dondurması uses wild orchid tubers as a thickening agent. The ice cream is able to stretch into a "rope" 60 cm (2 ft) long!

7 *Mantı*
These pasta packets are stuffed with minced lamb and served in a thin garlic sauce.

8 *Aşure*
Also known as Noah's pudding, this celebratory dish was first made by Mrs Noah, from the scraps remaining on the Ark at the end of the flood.

9 *Elma Çayı*
You may be offered this apple tea as an alternative to ordinary tea when visiting carpet shops.

10 *Rakı*
A clear spirit, *rakı* is usually an aniseed-based liquor similar to the Greek *ouzo* that is drunk after being diluted with water.

🔟 Restaurants

Alfresco dining at Asitane

1 Asitane
The complex flavours of Ottoman court cuisine are resurrected (based on extensive research) at Asitane *(see p79)*. Hundreds of years later, almond soup, melon stuffed with minced lamb and goose kebabs are still fit for a sultan.

2 İmroz
Established in 1941, this *(see p89)* is one of the liveliest, best-value *meyhanes* (taverns) on Nevizade Sokak. Go for the fixed-price menu.

3 Yeni Lokanta
One of the few Beyoğlu restaurants to attract well-heeled İstanbulites in from the suburbs, this stylish place *(see p89)* concentrates on good, solid Turkish dishes with a few modern twists. Book well in advance.

4 Seasons Restaurant
The Seasons *(see p67)* is the restaurant of the Four Seasons Hotel, which is set in a building that was once an Ottoman prison. Rather than thick walls, glass encloses the pretty garden in the court-yard. The modern

Seasons Restaurant

Mediterranean food on offer here is imaginative and delicious, and the service is attentive.

5 Feriye Lokantası
Situated in a 19th-century police station on the Bosphorus shore, this fashionable restaurant *(see p95)* takes a fresh look at Turkish cuisine, and combines traditional recipes with European flair to create one of the most exciting culinary experiences in the city.

6 Akdeniz Hatay Sofrası
This bustling place *(see p79)* serves up the best southeast Turkish food in the city. The tangy meze are excellent, the rice-stuffed chicken roasted in a salt crust and the metre-long kebabs a delight.

Akdeniz Hatay Sofrası

7 Mikla
Reserve a table on the terrace at the Marmara Pera Hotel's stylish rooftop restaurant Mikla *(see p89)*. Take in the perfect view of the Golden Horn – and the city below – as you dine. The Mediterranean cuisine offered here has Turkish and Nordic touches. The decor is elegant and there's even a swimming pool by the bar. Grab a cocktail and sink into one of the soft sofas as you listen to the DJ.

8 360
Rub shoulders with the swanky young set of Istanbul on the superb terrace

The terrace at 360

bar at 360 (see p88). Take your time to drink in the stunning views of both the Bosphorus and the Golden Horn, then withdraw to the spacious, well-lit interior to sample the eclectic delights on offer, which include samphire and soya sprouts, Vietnamese beef tartare, polenta-crusted calamari, seafood risotto, lamb loin confit, Margarita sorbet and pistachio baklava.

9 Balıkçı Sabahattin

Patrons can have a truly traditional Turkish experience at this wonderful fish restaurant (see p67), established in 1927 and situated in an old house with antique carpets and copper pots. There's also an outdoor terrace with lively Romani violinists. The food is excellent, although there is no menu – you choose from a wide range of meze and the catch of the day.

10 Giritli

Cretan dishes such as *ceviche*-style sea bass and cracked green olives cured in brine transport diners to their own little Greek island for the night. The fixed-price menu here (see p67) includes a selection of meze, perfectly prepared fish and unlimited glasses of wine. The restored historic house location and pretty restaurant garden are a definite bonus.

TOP 10 ENTERTAINMENT VENUES

1 Garaj Istanbul
MAP F1 ▪ Yeni Çarşı Cad 11/A, Beyoğlu ▪ (0212) 244 44 99 ▪ www.garajistanbul.org
An alternative performing arts venue, Garaj is housed in a former car park.

2 Hodja Pasha Cultural Centre
MAP T4 ▪ Hoca Paşa Hamam Sok 3, Sirkeci ▪ (0212) 511 46 26 ▪ www.hodjapasha.com
This Ottoman period bathhouse is great for folk and Whirling dervish shows.

3 Babylon
One of the best clubs (see p88) in town to enjoy rock and world music.

4 Cemal Reşit Rey Concert Hall
MAP B4 ▪ Darülbedayı Cad 1, Harbiye ▪ (0212) 232 98 30 ▪ www.crrkonsersalonu.org
Daily concerts include Western and Turkish classical, and world music.

5 Aksanat (Akbank) Cultural Centre
MAP L4 ▪ İstiklal Cad 8 ▪ (0212) 252 35 00 ▪ www.akbanksanat.com
This arts centre offers music and theatre.

6 Zorlu Centre
A performing arts centre (see p53), which hosts classical and pop concerts.

7 Ortaköy
This Bosphorus suburb (see p94) has some popular clubs (see p95) such as Anjelique and Blackk.

8 Nardis Jazz Club
Live jazz is performed in an intimate setting at this venue (see p88).

9 Süreyya Opera House
MAP U4 ▪ Bahariye Cad 29, Kadıköy ▪ (0216) 346 15 31
This Art-Deco-inspired 1920s theatre hosts opera and ballet.

10 Salon İKSV
Istanbul's top arts organization (see p88) hosts great classical and jazz concerts, plus theatre and film.

***Single City* play at Salon İKSV**

🔟 Shops and Markets

① Grand Bazaar
(Kapalı Çarşı)

One of the oldest, biggest and most exciting shopping malls in the world, the Grand Bazaar *(see pp22–3)* was set up to trade silk, spices and gold in the 15th century – and still sells all three, alongside jazzy glass lamp-shades, leather jackets and, of course, Turkish carpets.

Shops at the Grand Bazaar

② Spice Bazaar
(Mısır Çarşısı)

Also known as the Egyptian Bazaar *(see pp70–71)*, this is the best place in town to buy little presents, with a sea of spice stalls, piles of Turkish delight and plenty of cheap and cheerful souvenirs.

③ Çarşamba Street Market
(Çarşamba Pazarı)
MAP C3

So famous is this lively street market that the entire district is named Çarşamba (Wednesday) after the day of the week it is held. Many stalls are stacked with fruit, vegetables, cheeses, spices, dried fruit and nuts. Others concentrate on cheap clothing, while more traditional items include thin wooden rolling pins used to make flat breads, and brass coffee grinders. The sprawling market

stalls occupy several streets to the north and west of Fatih Mosque where the area is devoutly Muslim.

④ İstiklal Caddesi

The city's main modern shopping street, İstiklal *(see p86)* is packed day and night throughout the week. If you need a break from hunting for bargain designer clothes (in İş Merkezi) or vintage clothes in Syrian Passage (Suriye Pasajı), there are plenty of cafés to choose from.

⑤ Nişantaşı
MAP C4

Nişantaşı and neighbouring Teşvikiye are where local fashion-istas spend their money on a variety of international brands, including Versace and Dior.

⑥ Arasta Bazaar
(Arasta Çarşısı)

This small, upmarket bazaar *(see p64)* offers the best souvenir shopping in Sultanahmet. Originally built to provide money for the upkeep of the Blue Mosque, it sells good-quality carpets, jewellery and handicrafts in a relatively calm environment, conveniently close to many major sights and hotels.

Ceramic dishes in Arasta Bazaar

⑦ Caferağa Medresesi

Originally created by the great architect Sinan as a *madrasah* (theological school), this structure *(see p64)* is home to a variety of traditional craft shops producing and selling their wares.

8 Zorlu Centre
MAP C4 ▪ Koru Sokak, Zincirlikuyu ▪ (0850) 222 67 76
▪ www.zorlucenter.com

Designed by Turkey's leading architecture practice, Tabanlıoğlu, this state-of-the-art mall in a suburb overlooking the Bosphorus Bridge is worth seeing in its own right. It contains the PSM performance hall, a host of trendy shops and a high-tech cinema, as well as Istanbul Raffles Hotel.

The upmarket shopping mall, Kanyon

9 Kanyon, Levent
MAP U3

Join the city's most stylish shoppers at Kanyon, Istanbul's most architecturally distinctive shopping mall.

10 Çukurcuma, Galatasaray

Many travellers fall in love with this charming old quarter *(see p87)* of Beyoğlu, with its eclectic range of antiques and second-hand dealers, whose wares flow out onto the streets around Turnacıbaşı Sokağı. It is great for a morning's browsing.

Çukurcuma antique shop

(see p87)

TOP 10 THINGS TO BUY

Traditional glass bead jewellery

1 Jewellery
Precious metals are sold by weight, with a mark-up for workmanship. There are plenty of options, including designing your own jewellery.

2 Carpets
Carpets are the true glory of Turkish art – and you can have one on your own hall floor.

3 Leather
Jackets, bags, wallets and belts are great value and come in all styles, colours and qualities. Again, have your ideas custom-designed if you have enough time.

4 Clothes
Shop around and you can find good-quality clothes and great design at reasonable prices.

5 Textiles
Both cottons and silks are made here, and are reasonably priced. Silk scarves are a great-value present.

6 Spices
Great heaps of coloured spices are hard to resist. If you buy saffron, check it's the real thing – there's a cheaper alternative (safflower) on sale.

7 Historic Reproductions
Reproduction Ottoman miniatures are easy to carry and look great back at home.

8 Souvenirs
Shop for hand-woven towels and items hand-made from felt.

9 Blue Beads
The ubiquitous blue bead is actually a charm to ward off the "evil eye"; believe that or not, they make attractive gifts.

10 Food
Turkish delight, almonds and hazelnuts, pomegranate molasses and all sorts of other comestibles make great presents.

🔟 Istanbul for Free

1 Misir Apartment
MAP J5 ■ Istiklal Cad
163, Beyoğlu
This stylish Art Nouveau apartment block is home to a number of small but well-regarded art galleries, including Galeri Zilberman and Galerist. It's also worth heading up to the chic rooftop bar-restaurant, 360 (see p51). Here, you can enjoy a free panorama of Istanbul or treat yourself to a pricey drink.

2 Ottoman Mosques
One of Istanbul's greatest glories is its stunning array of domed Ottoman-era mosques, each flanked by one or more slender minarets. Many of the mosques have delightful interiors encrusted with pretty İznik tiles; all have that indefinable air of tranquillity and sanctity.

3 Park Life
With a population of at least 15 million, Istanbul can seem an incredibly congested city. Join the locals and escape to one of the city's green and historic parks. The best of these are Emirgan (see p94), Yıldız on the Bosphorus and Gülhane in the Old City.

Downtime in Gülhane Park

Church of St Anthony of Padua

4 Churches
Many Byzantine churches were turned into mosques during the Ottoman era, but the city retained a substantial Christian community until after World War I. Many are still in use and give a glimpse into the lives of a dwindling community. Try the Neo-Gothic Church of St Anthony of Padua (see p86) or the Greek Orthodox Church of St George (see p78).

5 Walking the Theodosian Walls
These 5th-century triple defences (see p42) saved Constantinople from Attila the Hun and many others for over 1,000 years. They have survived remarkably well, and walking their 6-km (4-mile) length from the Sea of Marmara north to the Golden Horn is a series of fascinating steps back into the past.

6 SALT Beyoğlu
MAP J5 ■ İstiklal Cad
163, Beyoğlu ■ (0212) 377 42 00
■ www.saltonline.org
This non-profitmaking gallery opened in a grand old 19th-century apartment block on bustling İstiklal Caddesi in 2011, and is now one of the city's premier exhibition spaces. There's also a café, bookshop, archive and library, and roof terrace.

7 Ottoman Bank Museum
MAP F3 ■ Bankalar Cad 11,
Karaköy ■ (0212) 334 22 00 ■ www.
saltonline.org
A trip to the immaculately preserved vaults of an iconic late Ottoman bank really brings to life what this most

cosmopolitan of neighbourhoods was like, with its Muslim Turks, Jews, Christian Armenians and Greeks. Pop upstairs to see a free exhibition in SALT Galata, sister branch to SALT Beyoğlu.

8 Koç Research Centre for Anatolian Civilizations
MAP J5 ■ Merkez Han, İstiklal Cad 181, Beyoğlu ■ (0212) 393 60 00 ■ www.rcac.ku.edu.tr/en

For well-presented exhibitions of an archaeological, historical or cultural nature, this ground-floor display space is just great. The centre is part of Koç University and has a well-stocked specialist library upstairs.

9 Şerefiye Cistern
MAP P4 ■ Piyer Loti Cad, Fatih

Constructed on the orders of Byzantine emperor Theodosius II, this compact and well-lit cistern was beautifully restored over a period of eight years. 32 marble columns topped by elaborately-carved capitals support the vaulted roof. Much like the Basilica cistern (see p63) this one is also connected to the Binbirdirek cistern (see p64).

Karaköy Fish Market

10 Karaköy Fish Market
MAP F3

Just west of the Galata Bridge in Karaköy is a small but authentic fish market; look out for the *hamsi* (anchovies) piled up in season. Walk west along the scruffy waterfront towards the Haliç metro bridge and admire the ferry-filled waters of the Golden Horn backed by the Old City's skyline of mosques and minarets.

TOP 10 BUDGET TIPS

Street food vendors in the city

1 Street Food
Street vendors sell cheap snacks, such as bagel-like *simits*, rice and chickpeas and *kokoreç* (stuffed lamb intestines).

2 Public Transport
www.istanbulkart.iett.gov.tr/en
The Istanbulkart saves up to 25 per cent per journey on public transport.

3 Entertainment
Numerous street entertainers and buskers perform on Beyoğlu's İstiklal Caddesi.

4 Alcohol
Restaurants that serve alcohol with meals are always more expensive.

5 Art Galleries
There are many free art galleries around İstiklal Caddesi, and street art in bohemian Galata.

6 Discounts
www.muzekart.com/en
For discounts on Istanbul's top sights, get a Museum Pass.

7 Clothing
For cheap clothes, try Beyoğlu İş Merkezi at İstiklal Cad 331, or Terkoz Çıkmaz İş Merkezi, off İstiklal Caddesi.

8 Bazaar
The streets surrounding the historic Spice Bazaar are better value than the market itself.

9 Ferries
Ferries up the Golden Horn or the Princes' Islands are as enjoyable, but cheaper, than the Bosphorus Cruise.

10 Nightlife
For a lively night at a *meyhane* (tavern), it is cheaper to get the all-inclusive deal with unlimited drinks.

🔟 Festivals and Events

Colourful display at Istanbul's Tulip Festival

❶ Tulip Festival
Apr ▪ Parks across the city

Turkey's national flower is the tulip *(lale)*. The tulip motif appeared endlessly on İznik tiles and today can be seen on Turkish Airlines aircraft. Each April millions of bulbs bloom across the city, with a competition to judge the best 100. Roadside verges become a riot of colour, but the flowers are best viewed in parks such as Emirgan and Gülhane.

❷ International Istanbul Film Festival
Apr ▪ (0212) 334 07 00 ▪ www. iksv.org

Since its inception in 1982, this festival has screened over 3,000 films from 76 countries. A highlight of the festival is the Award for Lifetime Achievement, instituted in 1996 – winners include French stars Alain Delon and Jeanne Moreau. Most screenings are held in cinemas around İstiklal Caddesi.

❸ Sugar Festival
(Şeker Ramazan Bayramı)
Three days, dates vary

The Sugar Festival marks the end of the month of Ramazan. People hand out sweets, visit relatives and enjoy cultural events – and Istanbul's bars and clubs are busy again. Many take advantage of the holiday period and head out of the city for a few days to escape the hustle and bustle.

❹ International Istanbul Music and Dance Festival
Jun ▪ (0212) 334 07 00 ▪ www.iksv.org

An impressive array of soloists, ensembles and orchestras has graced the stages of this prestigious festival since it was established in 1973. Mozart's opera The Abduction from the Seraglio is staged each year in Topkapı Palace.

❺ Conquest of Istanbul
May–Jun ▪ www.istanbul.gov.tr

Enjoy recreations of the siege of 1453, performances by the Ottoman Mehter military band, fireworks and much more during the Conquest celebrations. Festivities last a week, but the major spectacle usually takes place on May 29.

Conquest celebration procession

❻ International Istanbul Jazz Festival
Jun–Jul ▪ (0212) 334 07 00 ▪ www.iksv.org

The Jazz Festival's was established as an independent event in 1994. The musical range is broad, and you are as likely to encounter Björk or Elvis Costello as you are Brad Mehldau. The choice of venues is eclectic, with traditional clubs, outdoor stages and even a boat on the Bosphorus.

7 Feast of Sacrifice
(Kurban Bayramı)
Four days, dates vary

Also known as Eid-ul-Adha, the Feast of Sacrifice commemorates the Koranic version of Abraham's sacrifice. It falls two months and ten days after the end of Ramazan (Ramadan). Muslims celebrate the day by slaughtering a sheep on the morning of the first day of the festival. Friends and family are invited to a lavish meal, but much of the meat goes to charity. Note that this is Turkey's major annual public holiday – nearly everything closes, and public transport is seriously stretched.

 8 International Istanbul Fine Arts Biennial
Sep–Nov, every other year (odd numbers) ▪ **(0212) 334 07 00** ▪ **www.iksv.org**

Istanbul's Biennial showcases contemporary visual arts from Turkey and around the globe. Each festival is directed by a curator of a different nationality, who chooses a theme and arranges the programme of exhibitions, conferences and workshops. Since 2017 a work of art created for the festival is gifted to the city following the Biennial.

 9 International Puppet Festival
Oct–Nov ▪ **www.istanbulkukla festivali.com**

Karagöz, or Turkish Shadow Theatre, is a form of traditional Ottoman entertainment suitable for the whole family. Puppeteers come from as far as China to showcase their creations.

 10 Istanbul Marathon
Nov ▪ **Call ahead for tickets** ▪ **(0212) 453 30 00** ▪ **www.maraton. istanbul**

Every November, athletes have the chance to take part in the world's only transcontinental marathon with the Bosphorus Bridge closed for part of the day to allow those taking part to cross from Europe to Asia.

TOP 10 PUBLIC HOLIDAYS

Performance for Children's Day

1 New Year's Day
Istanbul rings in the new year with beautiful fireworks over the Bosphorus.

2 National Sovereignty and Children's Day
The nation celebrates the formation of the Turkish parliament and Children's Day on April 23.

3 International Workers' Day
A day for workers to call for their rights, May 1 is sometimes marred by violent protests.

4 Commemoration of Atatürk
The celebration of Atatürk's birthday coincides with the Youth and Sports Day on May 19. School children mark the day by marching through the streets.

5 Navy Day
Turkey's strong maritime forces are honoured on July 1.

6 Democracy and National Solidarity Day
Declared a holiday in 2016, July 15 marks the day of the failed coup by a part of the Turkish Armed Forces.

7 Armed Forces Day
Turkey's military, the largest armed force in NATO, is celebrated on August 26.

8 Victory Day
Turkey's victory over invading Greek forces in 1922 is celebrated on August 30.

9 Republic Day
On October 29, the public celebrates Atatürk's establishment of the Turkish republic in 1923.

10 Commemoration of the Death of Atatürk
One minute's silence is observed at 9:05am on November 10 in memory of Atatürk, who died on this day in 1938.

Istanbul
Area by Area

**Sunset views across the city to
Galata Tower from Topkapı Palace**

TOP10 Sultanahmet and the Old City

Egyptian Obelisk, Hippodrome

Many of the city's greatest sights are to be found in this historic area, which was in turn the centre of Byzantium, Constantinople and Ottoman Istanbul. Archaeologists have dated settlements in this strategic spot at the entrance to the Golden Horn to the 6th millennium BC, but recorded history begins around 667 BC, when Greek colonist Byzas founded Byzantion on Seraglio Point (now home to the Topkapı Palace). After his arrival in AD 324, Constantine transformed this port into the dazzling jewel of Constantinople, a new capital for the Roman Empire. By 1453, when the Ottomans seized power, the city was run-down and ruinous, and the new rulers stamped their authority – both religious and secular – on its buildings.

1 Haghia Sophia (Ayasofya)
Consecrated by Justinian in 537, the "Church of Holy Wisdom" is an enduring tribute to the skill of its architects, Anthemius of Tralles and Isidore of Miletus, who created a monument (see pp16–17) that has withstood wars and earthquakes. The scale of its vast central dome was not surpassed until the construction of St Peter's in Rome, 1,000 years later.

2 Hippodrome (At Meydanı)
MAP Q5
Now a peaceful park, the Hippodrome was once a Byzantine chariot race-track – a stadium capable of holding 100,000 people. Laid out in the 3rd century AD by Emperor Septimius Severus, it was enlarged and connected to the adjacent Great Palace by Constantine. There are three great monuments in the Hippodrome: the Egyptian Obelisk, the Obelisk of Theodosius (Dikilitaş), of c.1500 BC, which Theodosius transported from Luxor; the Serpentine Column (Yilanlı Sütun) from the Temple of Apollo at Delphi in Greece, made in 479 BC; and the Column of Constantine VII Porphryogenitus (Ormetaş), which is of unknown date and was named after the emperor who had it restored in the 10th century. The stadium once held four great bronze horses, but these were looted by the Crusaders in 1204 and can now be seen St Mark's Cathedral in Venice.

3 Blue Mosque (Sultanahmet Camii)
Begun in 1609, Sultan Ahmet I's mosque (see pp18–19) was built opposite Haghia Sophia and directly on top of Constantine's Great Palace to stress the supremacy of Islam and the Ottoman Empire over Christian Byzantium.

The impressive Blue Mosque

Museum of Turkish and Islamic Arts

④ Museum of Turkish and Islamic Arts

(Türk ve İslam Eserleri Müzesi)
MAP Q5 ■ At Meydanı Cad 46 ■ (0212)
518 18 05 ■ Open mid-Apr–Sep: 9am–
7pm daily; Oct–mid-Apr: 9am–5pm
daily ■ Adm ■ www.tiem.gov.tr

This museum is housed in the
palace built by İbrahim Paşa (c.1493–
1536), Grand Vizier to Süleyman the
Magnificent. It contains a collection
of more than 40,000 artifacts dating
from the 7th century to the present,
with exhibits of fine art, crafts and
Turkish domestic life in its evolution
from nomad's tent to modern home.

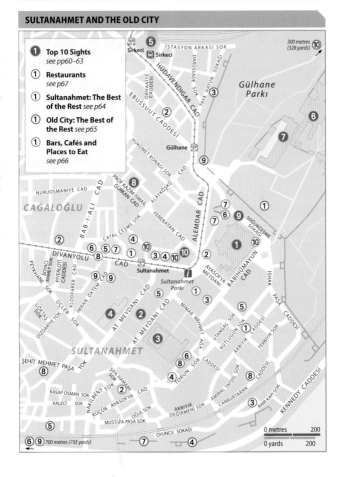

SULTANAHMET AND THE OLD CITY

❶	**Top 10 Sights** see pp60–63
①	**Restaurants** see p67
①	**Sultanahmet: The Best of the Rest** see p64
①	**Old City: The Best of the Rest** see p65
①	**Bars, Cafés and Places to Eat** see p66

Vibrant window, Sirkeci Station

5 Sirkeci Station
(Sirkeci Garı)

MAP R2 ■ İstasyon Arkasi Sok ■ (0212) 520 65 75 ■ Museum: open 9am–5pm Tue–Sat

Opened in November 1890, the glamorous eastern terminus for the *Orient Express* service was built by German architect August Jasmund in an eclectic style drawing together elements of Istanbul's varied architectural traditions. The station also houses a railway museum *(see p45)* and a modest restaurant. Since the opening of the Marmaray line in 2013 this grand old station is no longer the terminus for trains from Europe, but a mere stop on the metro – albeit the last one before the continent-linking Bosphorus Tunnel.

6 Topkapı Palace
(Topkapı Sarayı)

The great palace *(see pp12–13)* of the Ottoman Empire was both the residence and the centre of government of the early sultans. The whole complex can take a full day to explore; highlights include the Harem and the Treasury.

7 Archaeological Museum
(Arkeoloji Müzesi)

This *(see pp20–21)* is one of the world's great historical museums. It has three principal sections: the Museum of the Ancient Orient, which contains, among other things, the city gates of Babylon; the Tiled Kiosk, with a superb display of ceramics; and the main museum, where royal sarcophagi found at Sidon in Lebanon are star exhibits.

8 Cağaloğlu Baths
(Cağaloğlu Hamamı)

MAP Q3 ■ Prof Kazım İsmail Gürkan Cad 34 ■ (0212) 522 24 24 ■ Open for men: 8am–10pm daily; for women: 8am–8pm daily ■ Adm ■ www.cagaloglu hamami.com.tr

One of the city's best-known and most picturesque bathhouses, the Cağaloğlu Hamamı were built in 1741 by Sultan Mahmut I, with the intention of raising funds to support his library in Haghia Sophia. International and historical figures, from King Edward VIII and Florence Nightingale to Cameron Diaz and Harrison Ford, are all reputed to have bathed here. In more recent times, the baths have been used as a location for countless films and fashion shoots.

9 Soğukçeşme Sokağı
MAP R4

This steeply cobbled street, which runs between the outer walls of the Topkapı Palace and Haghia Sophia, is a sequence of pretty

---

SÜLEYMAN I

Known to the West as "the Magnificent", Süleyman I preferred the title Kanuni or "the law-giver". Taking the throne aged 26 in 1520, he ruled for 46 years. During that time, he doubled the size of the Ottoman Empire and, as caliph (supreme head of the Islamic faith), consolidated Sunni authority over Shia Islam. He also compiled the Codex Süleymanicus, a comprehensive legal system that defined the concept of justice, and guaranteed equal treatment for all. Süleyman was a great patron of the arts, as well as a poet and goldsmith.

Ottoman merchants' homes. The street was restored as part of a 1980s project that was one of the first of its kind in Istanbul. Nine of the houses form the Ayasofya Konakları (see p114), the city's first "special hotel", consisting of 64 guest rooms.

 Basilica Cistern
(Yerebatan Sarnıcı)
MAP R4 ▪ Yerebatan Cad 13 ▪ (0212) 512 15 70 ▪ Open 9am–5:30pm daily ▪ Adm ▪ www.yerebatan.com

Known as the "Sunken Palace" in Turkish, the structure was built as a vast underground water-storage tank. Begun by Constantine, it was expanded by Justinian in 532 to ensure that Constantinople was always supplied with water; covering an area of 9,800 sq m (105,000 sq ft), it once held about 80 million litres (18 million gallons). The cistern roof is supported by 336 pillars, 8 m (26 ft) in height. Look for the upside-down Medusa heads, reused from older buildings. This unusual tourist attraction is also popular as a film location and a venue for concerts. The cistern is undergoing restoration and parts of the structure may not be accessible to visitors.

Medusa head, Basilica Cistern

A DAY IN SULTANAHMET

▶ MORNING

Start your day at the dawn call of the *müezzin*, so that you are ready to visit the **Blue Mosque** (see pp18–19) as soon as it opens. From there, cross the square to **Haghia Sophia** (see pp16–17), then pay a visit to the **Basilica Cistern**, the **Hippodrome** (see p60) and the **Museum of Turkish and Islamic Arts** (see p61) before having a gentle stroll through the **Arasta Bazaar** (see p64) to the **Mosaic Museum** (see p64). This may sound like too much for a single morning, but the distance between each of these attractions is small, and most of the sites are fairly simple. You'll need a little time to relax after this, so choose one of the cafés or restaurants on **Divanyolu Caddesi** (see p64) for lunch.

AFTERNOON

Now choose one of two options: either walk across to the **Topkapı Palace** and spend the whole afternoon embroiled in Ottoman court intrigue, mayhem and murder; or wander through the side streets to the **Cağaloğlu Baths** for a Turkish bath before rejoining **Soğukçeşme Sokağı** and making your way to the vast **Archaeological Museum** (see pp20–21). When you've had your fill, continue down the hill for a peaceful stroll along the waterfront at **Eminönü** (see p70); then take the tram back up the hill to Sultanahmet and choose one of the many rooftop bars or restaurants from which to watch the sun set over the city and the floodlights playing on Haghia Sophia and the Blue Mosque.

See map on p61

Sultanahmet: The Best of the Rest

1 Sultanahmet Square
(Sultanahmet Meydanı)
MAP R4
Once the hippodrome of
Constantinople, this square
lies between the Haghia
Sophia (see pp16–17) and
Blue Mosque (see pp18–19).

2 The Milion Monument
(Milyon Taşı)
MAP R4 ■ Haghia Sophia
The marble pilaster of the Milion
can be found in the northern corner
of Sultanahmet Square. From the
4th century AD, it was used as
"point zero" for the measurement
of distances to the many cities of
the Byzantine Empire.

3 Baths of Roxelana
(Hürrem Sultan Hamamı)
MAP R5 ■ Ayasofya Meydanı
■ (0212) 517 35 35 ■ Open 8am–10pm
daily ■ www.ayasofyahamami.com
These baths were built for Süleyman
the Magnificent, and are named
after the sultan's apparently
scheming wife.

4 Great Palace Mosaic Museum
(Büyük Sarayı Mozaik Müzesi)
**MAP R6 ■ Arasta Bazaar ■ (0212) 518
12 05 ■ Open mid-Apr–Sep: 9am–7pm
daily (Oct–mid-Apr: until 4pm) ■ Adm**
Little remains of Emperor Justinian's
vast 6th-century palace except for
an elaborate mosaic floor.

Kaiser Wilhelm Fountain

Great Palace Mosaic Museum

5 Kaiser Wilhelm Fountain
MAP R5 ■ At Meydanı
German Emperor Wilhelm II
gifted this Neo-Byzantine
fountain to Sultan Abdül
Hamit II in 1901.

6 Arasta Bazaar
(Arasta Çarşısı)
**MAP R5 ■ Open 9am–
9pm daily**
The bazaar was originally
built to provide revenue for the Blue
Mosque. Today, there are around
40 shops selling carpets, textiles,
jewellery and other souvenirs.

7 Caferağa Medresesi
**MAP R4 ■ Caferiye Sok,
Soğukkuyu Çıkmazı 1 ■ (0212) 513
36 01 ■ Open 9am–7pm Mon–Sat**
Watch craftspeople create art, from
ceramics to calligraphy, in this 16th-
century Koranic college (see p52),
then take the product home or
sign up for a course.

8 Divanyolu Caddesi
MAP Q4
Divanyolu was once the Mese – the
main thoroughfare – of Byzantine
Constantinople and Ottoman
Istanbul, and continued all the
way to the Albanian coast.

9 Cistern of 1,001 Columns
(Binbirdirek Sarnıcı)
**MAP Q4 ■ Binbirdirek, İmran Öktem
Cad 4 ■ (0212) 518 10 01 ■ Open daily;
call ahead for timings ■ Adm ■ www.
binbirdirek.com**
There are only 224 columns in this
4th-century cistern. It houses several
cafés and hosts live music and events.

10 Carpet Museum
(Halı Müzesi)
**MAP S4 ■ Bab-ı Humayan Cad,
Sultanahmet ■ (0212) 512 69 93**
The old Ottoman soup kitchen near
Haghia Sophia is home to some of
Anatolia's oldest carpets and kilims.

Old City: The Best of the Rest

1 **Haghia Eirene**
(Aya İrini Kilisesi)
**MAP S4 ▪ Topkapı Palace
(1st courtyard)**
Built in the 6th century on the site of an earlier church, Haghia Eirene *(see p12)* was the city's cathedral until the construction of Haghia Sophia *(see pp16–17)*. Later an Ottoman arsenal, it is now a museum and used for concerts.

2 **Imperial Tombs**
MAP Q4 ▪ Divanyolu Cad
Designed by Garabet Balyan, the tombs of three of the last Ottoman sultans, Mahmut II, Abdül Aziz and Abdül Hamid II, lie beside busy Divanyolu in a peaceful graveyard.

3 **History of Islamic Science and Technology Museum**
MAP R2 ▪ Gülhane Park ▪ (0212) 528 80 65 ▪ Open 9am–5pm Wed–Mon ▪ Adm ▪ www.ibttm.org
Among the exhibits at this well-organized museum are fantastic models of scientific inventions.

4 **Sea Walls**
MAP M6–S6 ▪ Kennedy Cad
Believed to be built by Septimius Severus and extended by Theodosius *(see p77)*, the walls are best viewed from the main coastal road.

5 **Church of SS Sergius and Bacchus**
(Küçük Ayasofya Camii)
MAP P6 ▪ Küçük Ayasofya Camii Sok
Known as "Little Haghia Sophia", this church was built in 527 and converted into a mosque in 1500. The marble columns and carved frieze with a Greek inscription are all original.

6 **Kumkapı**
MAP M6
The old Byzantine harbour of Kumkapı *(see p67)* is now home to a plethora of lively fish restaurants.

7 **Bucoleon Palace**
MAP Q6 ▪ Kennedy Cad
Three vast marble windows stare sightlessly out to sea from this last standing fragment of the Great Palace, built into the sea wall.

Ruins of the Bucoleon Palace

8 **Sokollu Mehmet Paşa Mosque**
**MAP P5 ▪ Camii Kebir Sok
▪ Open daily (closed at prayer times)**
Built by Sinan for Grand Vizier Sokollu Mehmet Paşa, this lovely mosque behind the Hippodrome contains some fine İznik tiles, an elaborately painted ceiling and four tiny black stones from the Kaaba in Mecca. Visitors may need the keyholder to see inside the mosque.

9 **Review Pavilion**
(Alay Köşkü)
MAP R3 ▪ Topkapı Palace
Built into the outer walls of the Topkapı Palace, this small imperial pavilion overlooked the Sublime Porte, the entrance to the seat of government in later Ottoman times. Sultan İbrahim the Crazy took pot shots at passersby from here.

10 **Column of the Goths**
MAP S2 ▪ Gülhane Park
Erected to commemorate a great Roman victory over the Goths in the 3rd century, this fine 18-m-(60-ft-) high column is topped by an ornate Corinthian capital.

See map on p61

Bars, Cafés and Places to Eat

Customers relax in the laid-back Çorlulu Ali Paşa Medresesi

1 Çorlulu Ali Paşa Medresesi

MAP Q4 ■ Divanyolu Cad 36

Lounge on cushions in one of several atmospheric teashops with locals puffing on the *nargile*. No alcohol.

2 Doy-Doy

MAP Q5 ■ Sifa Hamamı Sok 13

This cheerful place has a good selection of kebabs, pizza, salads and vegetarian options. No alcohol.

3 Tahiri Sultanahmet Köftecisi

MAP Q4 ■ Divanyolu Cad 12

The speciality of this long-established institution is meatballs with bean salad and spicy tomato sauce. It has now been surrounded by other cafés with suspiciously similar names. Make sure you find the right one!

4 Lale Restaurant (Pudding Shop)

MAP Q4 ■ Divanyolu Cad 6

Once an essential stop on the "Hippy Trail", with a message board and copious quantities of cheap food, Lale is great for visitors. The food is good value, the service is friendly and they offer draught beer and free Wi-Fi.

5 Cozy Pub

MAP Q4 ■ Divan Yolu Cad 62

This spacious café-bar has a great location, beer and wine on tap and a wide range of pub fare, both Turkish and international.

6 Çaferağa Medresesi

MAP R4 ■ Caferiye Sokak

Enjoy a cup of coffee or opt for a light meal in the courtyard of this atmospheric, Sinan-designed *madrasah*, located near Haghia Sophia.

7 Çiğdem Pastanesi

MAP Q4 ■ Divanyolu Cad 62

Enjoy traditional Turkish tea or a well-made cappuccino at this classic patisserie. If you're in the mood for a light snack, the sticky, honey-drenched baklava is a local favourite.

8 Café Meşale

MAP R5 ■ Arasta Bazaar

A quiet place for a cup of tea and nargile during the day, in the evening Café Meşale becomes a restaurant with live music and Whirling dervish performances.

9 Terrace Istanbul

MAP Q4 ■ Arcadia Blue Hotel, Dr Imran Oktem Cad 1

This bar offers superb views of the Old City, Bosphorus, Sea of Marmara and hills of Asia.

10 Edebiyat Kıraathanesi

MAP R4 ■ Divan Yolu Cad 14

Under the management of the Turkish Literature Society, this refined café offers a staggering variety of traditional Turkish cakes and desserts, as well as quality coffees and teas.

Restaurants

PRICE CATEGORIES

For a typical meal of *meze* and main course for one without alcohol, and including taxes and extra charges.

....

₺ under ₺70 ₺₺ ₺70–120
₺₺₺ over ₺120

Appetizers, Seasons Restaurant

① Albura Kathisma
MAP R5 ■ Akbıyık Cad 38
■ (0212) 518 91 70 ■ ₺₺

One of the best on Akbıyık Street, this restaurant serves a good mix of Ottoman, Turkish and international dishes in atmospheric surroundings.

② Paşazade
MAP R3 ■ İbn-I Kemal Cad 13, Sirkeci ■ (0212) 513 37 57 ■ ₺₺

The best-value place to try recreations of Ottoman style dishes. The restaurant also has a variety of wines.

③ Giritli
MAP R6 ■ Keresteci Hakkı Sok 8 ■ (0212) 458 22 70 ■ ₺₺₺

Fine fish and a bountiful array of unusual *mezes* are the stars at this Cretan-style eatery.

Entrance to Giritli

④ Khorasani
MAP Q4 ■ Ticarethane Sok 39/41 ■ (0212) 519 5959 ■ ₺₺

Khorasani's southeast Turkish specialities are delicious, with the emphasis on freshly prepared kebabs cooked over charcoal.

⑤ Seasons Restaurant
MAP R5 ■ Four Seasons Hotel, Tevfikhane Sok 1
■ (0212) 402 30 00 ■ ₺₺₺

Top-class contemporary European cuisine with a hint of Asian fusion.

⑥ Amedros
MAP Q4 ■ Hoca Rüstem Sok 7, off Divanyolu ■ (0212) 522 83 56 ■ ₺₺

A bistro serving Turkish and European food, with good vegetarian options.

⑦ Matbah
MAP R4 ■ Ottoman Hotel Imperial, Caferiye Sok 6 ■ (0212) 514 61 51 ■ ₺₺₺

Tasty Ottoman and Turkish classics served in a lovely terrace restaurant.

⑧ Balıkçı Sabahattin
MAP R5 ■ Seyit Hasankuyu Sok 1, off Cankurtaran Cad ■ (0212) 458 18 24 ■ ₺₺₺

Established in 1927, this is one of the city's finest fish restaurants.

⑨ Kumkapı
MAP M6 ■ ₺₺

There are many *meyhanes* (taverns) to choose from in this old fishing neighbourhood, serving fresh fish and *meze* washed down with *rakı*. Musicians play traditional *fasıl* to the tables and expect to be tipped.

⑩ Mozaik Restaurant
MAP Q4 ■ İncirli Çavuş Sok 1, off Divanyolu ■ (0212) 512 41 77 ■ ₺₺

This popular restaurant serves a mix of Turkish and international favourites and is set in a restored 19th-century Ottoman house.

See map on p61

🔟 Bazaar Quarter and Eminönü

In 1453, after his conquest of Constantinople, Sultan Mehmet II chose this area, close to the Graeco-Roman Forum of the Bulls, as the place to begin construction of a model city based on Islamic principles. The key ingredients were mosques and *medreses* (religious schools), charitable institutions, accommodation for travellers, and a Grand Bazaar – the latter funding all the others and a great deal more besides. All these were constructed – and many still remain – in one of the city's most fascinating and vibrant districts, where you can buy, with equal ease, a plastic bucket and an antique silk carpet, an ancient religious text or a kilo of peppercorns.

Çemberlitaş Baths

BAZAAR QUARTER AND EMINÖNÜ

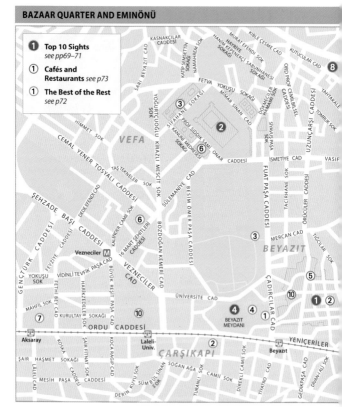

1. **Top 10 Sights** *see pp69–71*
1. **Cafés and Restaurants** *see p73*
1. **The Best of the Rest** *see p72*

Colourful ceramics, Grand Bazaar

1 Grand Bazaar
(Kapalı Çarşı)

The bazaar *(see pp22–3)* was one of the first institutions established by Mehmet the Conqueror after 1453. Its oldest part is the domed İç Bedesten, a lockable warehouse used for trading and storing the most valuable wares. Today, as well as covered streets containing thousands of shops and stalls, there are cafés, restaurants and teahouses. Several *hans* – originally travellers' inns – are now mostly workshops and small factories.

2 Süleymaniye Mosque Complex
(Süleymaniye Camii)

Built for Süleyman I in 1550–57, this mosque *(see pp26–7)* is the largest and most lavish in the city. Süleyman and his wife Roxelana are both buried here, while the great Mimar Sinan, architect of the mosque, is buried just outside the main complex in a tomb he designed and built himself.

3 Çemberlitaş Baths
(Çemberlitaş Hamamı)

Nurbanu, wife of the drunken Selim the Sot (son of Süleyman and Roxelana), commissioned these baths *(see pp30–31)* from Sinan in 1584. In those days, they were run as a charitable foundation; today they are distinctly more upmarket. Their gracious domed halls make them a popular tourist attraction.

4 Beyazıt Square
(Beyazıt Meydanı)

MAP M3

This grand open space has been one of the city's principal meeting places for centuries. Popularly known as Beyazıt Square, its official name is Freedom Square (Hürriyet Meydanı). It stands on the site of the late Roman Forum Tauri (Forum of the Bulls), which was extended by Emperor Theodosius in 393. The forum gained its name from the bronze bull at its centre, a place of sacrifice in the pre-Christian era. Some of its colonnades were reused in the building of the Basilica Cistern *(see p63)*, while others lie abandoned along the tram tracks on Ordu Caddesi. The square is home to the Beyazıt Mosque and Istanbul University.

Galata Bridge facing the New Mosque at sunset

5 Galata Bridge
(Galata Köprüsü)
MAP F3

The predecessor of this modern bridge across the Golden Horn was an iron pontoon structure of 1909–12. It was underequipped for modern traffic and was replaced in 1994 by the current two-level concrete bridge. The city views from the lower level, especially at sunset, are breath-taking. Parts of the old bridge, further up the Golden Horn near Ayvansaray, have been re-erected.

6 Constantine's Column
(Çemberlitaş)
MAP P4 ■ Divanyolu Cad

Built of Egyptian porphyry, this column, 35 m (115 ft) tall, once stood in the centre of the Forum of Constantine. It was erected as part of the inauguration of the Roman Empire's new capital in 330. Constantine buried holy relics – said to have included the axe Noah used to build his ark – around the base. Its Turkish name, Çemberlitaş (Hooped Column), refers to the reinforcing metal hoops added in 416 and replaced in the 1970s.

7 Eminönü
MAP N1

From the Grand Bazaar, steep alleys crowded with market stalls lead down through Tahtakale to the Eminönü waterfront. It's a great place to roam, with mosques and markets, Ottoman warehouses, street sellers offering everything from *simits* to fake watches, and a bank of piers with ferries to every part of the city, all split by the swirl of traffic along the dual carriageway that leads around the coast.

8 Rüstem Paşa Mosque
(Rüstem Paşa Camii)
MAP N1 ■ Mahkeme Sok ■ (0212) 526 73 50 ■ Open 9am–dusk daily

Tile detail, Rüstem Paşa Mosque

This enchanting mosque was built by Sinan in 1561. It was commissioned by Süleyman the Magnificent's daughter Mihrimah in memory of her husband, Rüstem Paşa, Süleyman's Grand Vizier. The mosque blazes with richly coloured İznik tiles, inside and out, while galleries and windows flood the hall with light.

9 Spice Bazaar
(Mısır Çarşısı)
MAP P1 ■ Eminönü ■ Open 8am–7:30pm daily

This marketplace was built in 1660 as part of the New Mosque complex. Its Turkish name (Egyptian Bazaar) derives from the fact that it was orig-inally financed by duties on Egyptian imports, although it is better known in English as the Spice Bazaar because, for centuries, spices were the main goods sold here. These days, the bazaar has turned into a major tourist attraction. The bazaar, and the streets around it, are the best places to buy small presents, from *lokum* (Turkish delight) and phials of saffron, to pistachios, almonds, incense and coffee.

⑩ New Mosque
(Yeni Cami)

MAP P1 ■ Eminönü ■ (0212) 512 23 20 ■ Open 9am–dusk daily

This large, rather gloomy mosque was commissioned in 1597 by Valide Sultan Safiye, mother of Sultan Mehmet III. Work was interrupted when the architect was executed for heresy and Safiye was banished after her son's death. It was completed in 1663 by Valide Sultan Turhan Hatice, mother of Sultan Mehmet IV. The interior is richly decorated but has relatively poor-quality İznik tiles.

Facing the mosque are the tombs of Valide Sultan Turhan Hatice, Mehmet IV, five other sultans and many princes and princesses.

Façade, New Mosque

EMPEROR CONSTANTINE

The son of a leading army officer, Constantine (c.272–337) became one of a triumvirate of rulers of the Roman Empire. In 312, following a religious vision, he defeated his main rival, Maxentius, while fighting under the sign of the Christian cross. On becoming sole emperor in 324, he declared Christianity the state religion. In 325, he called the Council of Nicaea, which laid down the basic tenets of the faith. In 330, he inaugurated his new capital, Constantinople. On his deathbed, he formally converted to Christianity, and was buried at the city's Church of the Holy Apostles (see p75).

A DAY'S SHOPPING

▶ MORNING

Start the day clean and refreshed after a visit to the **Çemberlitaş Baths** (see p69), then pop into the **Nuruosmaniye Mosque** (see p72) before getting down to the real business of the day in the **Grand Bazaar** (see p69). Take a break at one of the cafés in the bazaar and enjoy a coffee, then walk on through **Beyazıt Square** (see p69) and down the hill to **Süleymaniye Mosque** (see p69) to pay your respects at the tombs of Süleyman and Roxelana. A good option for lunch is the **Darüzziyafe** restaurant (see p73), or try one of the cafés next to the mosque.

AFTERNOON

Leave the mosque along İsmetiye Caddesi, turn left into Uzunçarşı Caddesi and head down the hill through crowded market streets, where metal- and woodworkers still ply their trade, before turning right on **Tahtakale Caddesi**, a sensory treat with its traditional spice and coffee sellers. Carry on downhill and eventually you will end up in Eminönü, where you can visit the **Rüstem Paşa Mosque** and look at the **New Mosque** before a last round of shopping – if you have the stamina – in the **Spice Bazaar**. Between the New Mosque and the Spice Bazaar is the market for flowers, plants, seeds and songbirds. Have dinner at **Hamdi Et Lokantası** (see p73) or Paşazade near Sirkeci Station (see p67) – or take the tram back up to Sultanahmet and choose a rooftop bar or restaurant from which to enjoy sunset views.

See map on pp68–9 ←

The Best of the Rest

1 Second-Hand Book Bazaar (Sahaflar Çarşısı)

MAP M4 ▪ Sahaflar Çarşısı Sok

Manuscripts have been traded in this courtyard since medieval times, although printed books were banned until 1729. Academic textbooks and coffee table books on Turkey are now predominately sold here.

2 Arch of Theodosius

MAP M4 ▪ Beyazıt Meydanı

A jumble of massive, fallen columns litter the side of the road in Beyazıt Square, all that remains of the 4th-century triumphal Arch of Theodosius. The similarly carved columns in the Basilica Cistern *(see p63)* were clearly taken from here.

3 Beyazıt Tower (Beyazıt Kulesi)

MAP M3 ▪ Off Fuat Paşa Cad ▪ Closed to the public

This elegant marble tower, built in 1828 as a fire lookout, is in the Istanbul University grounds.

4 Beyazıt Mosque (Beyazıt Camii)

MAP M4 ▪ Ordu Cad ▪ (0212) 212 09 22

Built in 1506 for Beyazıt II, this is the oldest surviving imperial mosque in Istanbul.

The towering Laleli Mosque

5 Atik Ali Paşa Mosque (Atik Ali Paşa Camii)

MAP P4 ▪ Yeniçeriler Cad

This 15th-century copy of the original Fatih Mosque is named after its builder, Grand Vizier to Beyazıt II.

6 Kalenderhane Mosque (Kalenderhane Camii)

MAP E5 ▪ 16 Mart Şehitleri Cad ▪ Open daily (closed at prayer times)

Built on the site of a 5th-century bathhouse, it was remodelled in the 12th century as the Church of Theotokus Kyriotissa and then into a mosque. Don't miss the superb Byzantine marble in the prayer hall.

7 Laleli Mosque (Laleli Cami)

MAP D5 ▪ Ordu Cad ▪ Open prayer times only

The Laleli Mosque was built by Mustafa III in 1763, with lavish use of coloured marble in the new Ottoman Baroque style. Mustafa is buried here.

8 Nuruosmaniye Mosque (Nuruosmaniye Cami)

MAP P4 ▪ Vezirhanı Cad

Completed by Sultan Osman III in 1755, Nuruosmaniye was the first Ottoman Baroque mosque in the city. The mosque is part of a larger complex that includes an Islamic school and a library.

Beyazıt Tower

9 Hodja Pasha Cultural Centre

MAP Q2 ▪ Hoca Paşa Hamam Sok 3, Sirkeci ▪ (0212) 511 46 26

This restored bathhouse forms a superb setting for Whirling dervishes.

10 Istanbul University

MAP M2–3 ▪ Beyazıt Meydanı ▪ (0212) 512 52 57

Turkey's oldest higher education institution, the university moved to its present campus in 1866. Security is very tight, but it is usually possible to take a walk through the grounds during the working week.

Cafés and Restaurants

① Pandeli
MAP P1 ▪ Mısır Çarşısı 1
▪ (0212) 527 39 09 ▪ ₺₺₺

Set in a domed, İznik-tiled dining room above the Spice Market, Pandeli has been an Istanbul institution since it opened in 1901. Book in advance.

② Bedestan Café
MAP N3 ▪ Cevahir Bedesteni 143–151, Kapalı Çarşı ▪ (0212) 520 22 50 ▪ ₺

The most tasteful café in the Grand Bazaar *(see pp22–3)*, with snacks and both Turkish and international coffee.

③ Darüzziyafe
MAP M1 ▪ Şifahane Cad 6
▪ (0212) 511 84 14 ▪ ₺₺

Once the soup kitchen of the Süleymaniye Mosque Complex, this atmospheric restaurant serves first-rate Ottoman food. No alcohol.

④ Nar Lokanta
MAP P3 ▪ Armaggan, Nuruosmaniye Cad 65 ▪ (0212) 522 28 00 ▪ ₺₺

An organic version of the traditional Turkish *lokanta*, and great for lunch.

Refreshments at Şark Kahvesi

⑤ Şark Kahvesi
MAP N3 ▪ Yağlıkçılar Cad 134
▪ (0212) 512 11 44 ▪ ₺

This atmospheric café is a popular tea and coffee spot.

PRICE CATEGORIES
For a typical meal of *meze* and main course for one without alcohol, and including taxes and extra charges.
....
₺ under ₺70 ₺₺ ₺70–120
₺₺₺ over ₺120

⑥ Tarihi Süleymaniyeli Kurufasulyeci
MAP M2 ▪ Süleymaniye Cad, Prof Siddik Sami Onar Cad 11 ▪ (0212) 513 62 19 ▪ No credit cards ▪ ₺

This restaurant has been serving simple Ottoman cuisine for 80 years. Try the slow-cooked rice and beans.

⑦ Kahve Dünyası
MAP P4 ▪ Nuruosmaniye Cad 79 ▪ (0212) 527 32 82 ▪ ₺

Close to the Grand Bazaar, this is a branch of the popular Turkish coffeehouse chain.

⑧ Hamdi Et Lokantası
MAP P1 ▪ Kalçın Sok 17, Eminönü ▪ (0212) 528 03 90 ▪ ₺₺₺

Specialities here include *erikli kebap* (minced suckling lamb).

⑨ Surplus
MAP E3 ▪ Zindan Han, Ragıp GümüşPala Cad 54 ▪ (0212) 513 37 57 ▪ ₺₺₺

Offering great views over the city and Galata with an excellent choice of Ottoman dishes and good wines.

⑩ Havuzlu Lokantası
MAP N3 ▪ Gani Çelebi Sok 3, Kapalı Çarşı ▪ (0212) 527 33 46 ▪ Closed dinner, Sun ▪ ₺

The best of the simple restaurants in the covered bazaar, this place offers excellent kebabs and *meze*. Arrive early as the restaurant can get crowded.

See map on pp68–9 ←

TOP 10 The Golden Horn, Fatih and Fener

Mosaic, Church of Pammakaristos

The Golden Horn, a fjord-like river inlet that divides the old and new cities of European Istanbul, is enjoying a new lease of life. Often overlooked by visitors, this part of Istanbul is dotted with historic attractions. Of these the Church of St Saviour in Chora stands out and is equal to anything on the Historic Peninsula itself. Fener and Balat are now prime real-estate locations and popular settings for television programmes. The Old City shoreline has miles of narrow parks and walkways and the new city shore is home to attractions such as Miniatürk and the Rahmi Koç Museum.

THE GOLDEN HORN, FATIH AND FENER

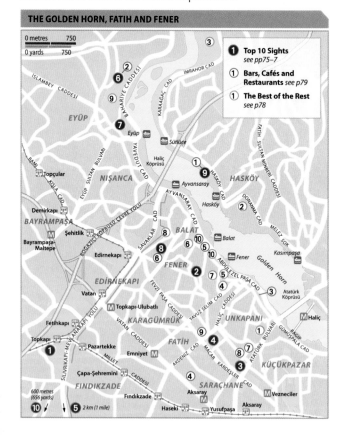

1 Top 10 Sights
see pp75–7

1 Bars, Cafés and Restaurants see p79

1 The Best of the Rest
see p78

1 Panorama 1453

MAP A5 ▪ Topkapı Kültür Parkı, Topkapı ▪ (0212) 415 14 53 ▪ Open 9am–5pm daily ▪ Adm ▪ www. panoramikmuze.com

Situated right by the Theodosian Walls (see p42), this history museum vividly recreates the moment in 1453 when the walls were finally breached. Painted on the inside of a large dome are some 10,000 life-like figures replaying the desperate Byzantine defence against the besieging Ottoman Turks. Take a seat in the museum's helicopter simulator for a bird's-eye view of Istanbul or a historical tour around the country.

The historic Aqueduct of Valens

2 Church of Pammakaristos (Fethiye Camii)

MAP K3 ▪ Fethiye Kapısı Sok ▪ Open 9am–5pm daily ▪ Adm

Built by Emperor John II Comnenus in the 12th century, this was the headquarters of the Greek Orthodox Patriarchate from 1456 to 1568. It was later converted into a mosque, and in 1573 renamed Fethiye (Victory) to celebrate Murat III's conquest of present-day Georgia and Azerbaijan. The side-chapel is a museum, containing some of the finest Byzantine mosaics in Istanbul. The church is under restoration and may be closed.

3 Aqueduct of Valens (Bozdoğan Kemeri)

MAP D4 ▪ Atatürk Bulvarı (north side of Saraçhane Parkı)

West of Süleymaniye are the remains of the two-storey aqueduct built by Emperor Valens in 368. Repaired many times in the intervening years, it remained in use until the 19th century, bringing water from the Belgrade Forest to the centre of the Great Palace complex.

4 Fatih Mosque (Fatih Camii)

MAP C3–4 ▪ Fevzi Paşa Cad ▪ Open 9am–dusk daily

This huge Baroque mosque (see p40) is the third building to have occupied this site. The first was the Church of the Holy Apostles (burial place of many Byzantine emperors, including Constantine). Mehmet the Conqueror then constructed Istanbul's first purpose-built imperial mosque here, but it was destroyed in an earthquake in 1766. Today's mosque was built mainly in the 18th century by Sultan Mustafa III. The grounds contain the tombs of Mehmet the Conqueror and his wife Gülbahar Hatun. There is a colourful market in the surrounding streets on Wednesdays.

Fatih Mosque

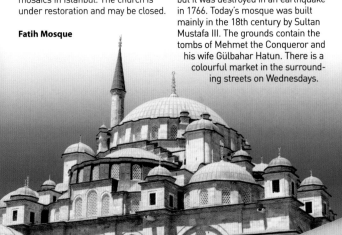

The vast grounds of Yedikule Castle

⑤ Yedikule Castle (Yedikule Hisarı)

MAP A6 ■ Yedikule Meydanı Sok

This seven-tower Ottoman fortress is built onto a section of the Theodosian Walls *(see p42)*. Built within its outer walls is the Golden Gate, a triumphal arch constructed by Emperor Theodosius I in 390. Note that the Walls are not safe to visit alone and the castle is not open to the public.

View from the Pierre Loti Café

⑥ Pierre Loti

During his time in Istanbul, Pierre Loti – the pseudonym and nom de plume of French sailor, author and Turkophile Julien Viaud – frequented a café in Eyüp, and the surrounding area is now named after him. Arriving in the city in 1876, Viaud fell in love with a local woman whose name he gave to the title of his novel, *Aziyade*, which chronicles their difficult relationship. The area known as Pierre Loti Hill can be visited via the cable car beside Eyüp Mosque. The hilltop Pierre Loti Café *(see p79)* affords splendid views of the Golden Horn.

⑦ Eyüp Sultan Mosque (Eyüp Sultan Camii)

MAP A4 ■ Eyüp Meydanı (off Camii Kebir Cad) ■ (0212) 564 73 68 ■ Tomb: open 9:30am–4:30pm ■ Donations

Istanbul's holiest mosque was built by Mehmet the Conqueror in 1458, over the *türbe* (burial site) of the Prophet Mohammed's friend and standard-bearer, Eyüp el-Ensari, whose tomb opposite is one of the holiest pilgrimage sites in Islam (after Mecca and Jerusalem). The mosque courtyard has intricately painted İznik tiles, and is usually filled with worshippers queuing to pay their respects.

⑧ Church of St Saviour in Chora (Kariye Camii)

First a church, then a mosque, and now a museum, the Church of St Saviour in Chora *(see pp28–9)* was rebuilt in the late 11th century and restored in the early 14th by Theodore Metochites, who also commissioned the superb series of mosaics and frescoes that he hoped would secure him "a glorious memory among posterity till the end of the world".

⑨ Rahmi Koç Museum (Rahmi Koç Müzesi)

MAP A5 ■ Hasköy Cad 5 ■ (0212) 369 66 00 ■ Open 10am–5pm Tue–Fri; Apr–Sep: 10am–7pm Sat & Sun; Oct–Mar: 10am–6pm Sat & Sun ■ Adm ■ www.rmk-museum.org.tr

This eclectic museum is named after its founder, the industrialist Rahmi Koç. The main part of the collection, which includes an assortment of vintage cars, is situated in a 19th-century shipyard building. Outside are aircraft, boats, restored shops and a submarine. Across the road, in a restored Ottoman anchor foundry with Byzantine foundations, are model engines, trains, cars and more boats. There is also an excellent café *(see p79)* and the gourmet Halat Restaurant.

Vintage car

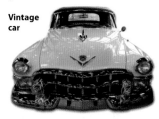

⑩ Church of St Mary of the Spring
(Zoodochus Pege Silivrikapı)
MAP A6 ■ Seyit Nizam Cad 3
■ Open 8:30am–4:30pm daily

Set amidst Christian and Muslim cemeteries, this Greek Orthodox church *(see p46)* was built in 1833 on the site of an older church. It is famous for its *ayazma* or sacred spring, which is full of fish, and located beneath the church.

BUILT TO LAST

There were 10 fortified gates and 192 towers in the Theodosian Walls. The outer wall is 2-m (6-ft) thick and 8.5-m (28-ft) tall, separated from the 5-m (16-ft-) thick, 12-m- (39-ft-) high inner wall by a 20-m (66-ft) moat **(below)**. The walls of Byzantium were built to withstand anything, and did so for 1,000 years. When they were breached in 1453, the last Byzantine Emperor, Constantine XI, vanished into history, last seen fighting on the wall itself.

A DAY ALONG THE GOLDEN HORN

▶ MORNING

Take the Haliç ferry from near the Galata Bridge to Eyüp, then ride the cable car up the tree-clad cemetery hill. Enjoy tea at **Pierre Loti Café** *(see p79)* before heading down through the cemetery to queue at the tomb of Eyüp Ensarı in the **Eyüp Sultan Mosque**. Stroll down the Golden Horn to join the line of the **Theodosian Walls** *(see p42)*. Turn south and walk alongside the mighty walls as they march uphill to the **Palace of the Porphyrogenitus** *(see p78)*. Deviate slightly from the line of the walls to visit the Byzantine **Church of St Saviour in Chora**, with its superb mosaics and frescoes. Right next to the church the **Asitane Restaurant** *(see p79)* serves up delicious Ottoman Turkish dishes in a leafy garden.

AFTERNOON

Continue south along the line of the walls, admiring the defences which kept the city's enemies at bay for centuries. The first high-light en route is the **Mihrimah Mosque**, spectacularly situated on the Old City's highest hill. About halfway along the length of the walls is **Panorama 1453** *(see p75)*, with its recreation of the famous siege of 1453. Continue downhill to **Yedikule Fortress**, a massive Ottoman-era fortress incorporating part of the Theodosian walls and the legendary Golden Gate. The total length of the walk is around 6 km (4 miles); ride the metro back to the centre from the Kazlıçeşme stop.

See map on p74 ←

The Best of the Rest

1 Church of the Pantocrator
(Molla Zeyrek Camii)

MAP D3 ■ İbadethane Sok, Küçükpazar ■ (0212) 532 50 23 ■ Bus 28, 61B, 87 ■ Open 20 mins before and after prayer times ■ Small tips welcomed

This 12th-century Byzantine church was converted into a mosque in 1453.

2 Aynalıkavak Palace
(Aynalıkavak Kasrı)

MAP D1 ■ Aynalıkavak Cad, Hasköy ■ (0212) 256 95 70 ■ Bus 47, 54 ■ Open 9am–5pm daily except Mon & Thu ■ Adm

This 17th-century Ottoman palace has an interesting exhibition of Turkish musical instruments.

Miniature models at Miniatürk

3 Miniatürk

MAP A4 ■ İmrahor Cad, Sütlüce ■ Bus 47C, 47E ■ Ferry Haliç to Sütlüce ■ Open 9am–6pm daily ■ Adm ■ www.miniaturk.com.tr

This intriguing park contains 1:25 scale models of the country's most impressive structures, from the Bosphorus Bridge to Haghia Sophia.

4 Yavuz Selim Mosque
(Yavuz Selim Camii)

MAP C3 ■ Yavuz Selim Cad, Fatih ■ Bus 90 ■ Tomb: open 9am–5pm

This elegant 16th-century mosque was built to honour Selim I, who doubled the size of the Ottoman Empire. His tomb is in the garden.

5 Church of St George
(Ortodoks Parikhanesi)

MAP L3 ■ Sadrazam Ali Paşa Cad 35, Fener ■ (0212) 525 54 16 ■ Bus 55T, 99A ■ Open 9am–5pm daily

This church (see p40) is the spiritual centre of the Orthodox Church community worldwide.

6 Balat

MAP K2 ■ Synagogue: Gevgili Sok ■ (0212) 244 19 80 ■ Bus 55T, 99A ■ Open by appointment

Balat was once home to the city's Sephardic Jewish community. Visit the 15th-century Ahrida Synagogue, which is one of the oldest in Istanbul.

7 Church of St Mary of the Mongols (Kanlı Kilise)

MAP L3 ■ Tevkii Cafer Mektebi Sok, Fener ■ (0212) 521 71 39 ■ Bus 55T, 99A ■ Ring on the compound door for entry

This church (see p41) was built by Maria Palaeologina, a Byzantine princess who married a Mongol khan, and later became a nun.

8 Palace of the Porphyrogenitus
(Tekfur Sarayı)

MAP J1 ■ Şişhane Cad, Edirnekapı ■ Bus 87, 90, 126 ■ Ferry Haliç to Ayvansaray ■ Groups only, by appointment with Haghia Sophia

Once an annexe of the Blachernae Palace, it has recently been restored.

9 Eyüp Cemetery

MAP A4 ■ Camii Kebir Sok ■ Bus 39, 55T, 99A ■ Ferry Haliç to Eyüp

A steep walk leads past hundreds of Ottoman-era gravestones. There's a superb view of the Golden Horn.

10 Church of St Stephen of the Bulgars
(Bulgar Kilisesi)

MAP D2 ■ Mürsel Paşa Cad 85, Balat ■ Bus 55T, 99A ■ Open 9am–5pm daily

This late 19th-century church was prefabricated in Vienna, in cast iron.

Bars, Cafés and Restaurants

PRICE CATEGORIES

For a typical meal of *meze* and main course for one without alcohol, and including taxes and extra charges.

₺ under ₺70 ₺₺ ₺70–120
₺₺₺ over ₺120

Calamari dish at Asitane Restaurant

1 Café du Levant, Sütlüce
■ MAP A4 ■ Hasköy Cad 5
■ (0212) 369 66 07 ■ ₺₺

This café is located in the Rahmi Koç museum *(see p76)* and serves Gallic cuisine.

2 Pierre Loti Café, Eyüp
■ MAP A4 ■ Gümüşsuyu Karyağdı Sok 5 ■ (0212) 497 13 13 ■ ₺

The interior of this hilltop café has traditional tiles, tea-making paraphernalia and exhibits relating to the novelist Pierre Loti *(see p76)*. Outside, the shady terrace offers fine views of the Goldern Horn.

3 Cibalikapı Balıkçısı, Fener
■ MAP E3 ■ Kadir Has Cad 5
■ (0212) 533 28 46 ■ ₺₺

This traditional tavern serves fresh fish of the day and a wonderful selection of hot and cold *meze*. Lively and informal with good views of the Golden Horn.

4 Akdeniz Hatay Sofrası, Fatih
■ MAP A6 ■ Ahmediye Cad 44/A, Aksaray ■ (0212) 444 72 47 ■ ₺

Choose from a vast array of *meze*, tender kebabs and specialities, including chicken roasted in a salt crust at this establishment.

5 Köfteci Arnavut, Balat
■ MAP L2 ■ Mürselpaşa Cad 139
■ (0212) 531 66 52 ■ ₺

Serving up *köfte* (meatballs) since 1947, this little eatery is perfect for a traditional Turkish lunch. The doors close when the *köfte* run out, usually by mid-afternoon, so get there early.

6 Asitane Restaurant, Edirnekapı
■ MAP J2 ■ Kariye Oteli, Kariye Camii Sok 6 ■ (0212) 635 79 97 ■ ₺₺₺

Dishes with delicate Ottoman flavours are served in a classy setting, with a summer courtyard. Reservations are recommended.

7 Sur Ocakbaşı, Fatih
■ MAP C4 ■ Itfaye Cad 27
■ (0212) 533 80 88 ■ ₺₺

A delight for meat lovers, this place serves spicy, meat-topped *lahmacun* (Turkish pizza) and kebabs in the shadow of the Aqueduct of Valens *(see p75)*.

8 Siirt Şeref Büryan, Fatih
■ MAP C4 ■ Itfaye Cad 4 ■ (0212) 635 80 85 ■ ₺₺

An authentic eatery specializing in *perde pilaf*, a delicious pilau rice cooked in pastry, and *büryan*, lamb slow-cooked in a clay pit. No alcohol.

9 Kömür, Fatih
■ MAP J3 ■ Fevziy Paşa Cad 18
■ (0212) 631 40 04 ■ ₺

Locals flock to this simple café for delicious and ultra-cheap self-service dishes of Black Sea food.

10 Sahil Restoran, Balat
■ MAP K3 ■ Mürselpaşa Cad 245
■ (0212) 525 61 85 ■ ₺₺

A good-value tavern where visitors can enjoy the aniseed spirit *rakı* alongside *meze* and fresh fish.

See map on p74

TOP10 Beyoğlu

Gold shield in the Military Museum

Set on a steep hill north of the Golden Horn, facing the old town of Stamboul, is the "new town" of Beyoğlu, previously known as Pera – simply, "the other side". The area is hardly "new"; there has been a settlement here for 2,000 years. In the early Byzantine era, Pera was populated by Jewish merchants. In the late 13th century, Genoese merchants were given Galata as a reward for helping the Byzantines recapture the city from the Crusaders. In Ottoman times, European powers established embassies and trading centres, and Istanbul's commercial centre shifted here from the Grand Bazaar area. Today, Beyoğlu is the heart of modern European Istanbul, its streets (such as pedestrianized İstiklal Caddesi) lined with consulates, churches, stylish bars and all the latest shops.

1 Galata Tower
(Galata Kulesi)

MAP F2 ■ Büyük Hendek Sok ■ (0212) 293 81 80 ■ Viewing platform: open 9am–7pm daily (dinner show from 8pm–1am) ■ Adm

One of the city's most distinctive sights, the 67-m- (220-ft-) high tower was built in 1348 by the Genoese, the Byzantine Empire's greatest trading partners, as part of their fortification of Galata. Since then, the tower has survived several earthquakes, and been restored many times. A lift climbs eleven floors to the top where there is a viewing balcony, nightclub and restaurant – views of the Golden Horn and the city are fabulous. In the evenings, the restaurant hosts a dinner and cabaret with Turkish folk dance and belly dancing *(see p88)*.

Galata Tower

Previous pages The Golden Horn as seen from Galata Tower

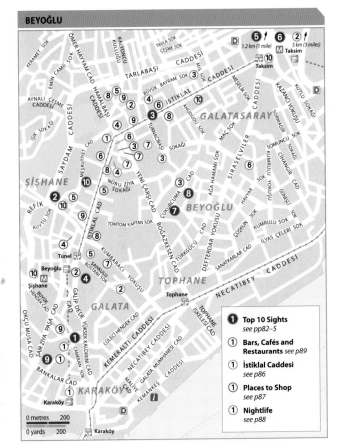

BEYOĞLU

1 Top 10 Sights
see pp82–5

1 Bars, Cafés and
Restaurants see p89

1 İstiklal Caddesi
see p86

1 Places to Shop
see p87

1 Nightlife
see p88

0 metres   200
0 yards   200

2 Pera Palace Hotel
(Pera Palas Oteli)

Opened in 1892 mainly for travellers arriving on the *Orient Express*, the Pera Palace *(see p114)* is Istanbul's most famous hotel. British thriller writer Agatha Christie stayed here often between 1924 and 1933 and is said to have written *Murder on the Orient Express* in Room 411. Over the years, the hotel has also been frequented by well-known figures such as Mata Hari, Leon Trotsky, Greta Garbo and Atatürk, the "Father of the Turks" *(see p33)*. In 1981, the Atatürk Museum was opened in the great leader's favourite room in the hotel, No. 101. The exhibit displays many of his personal items.

3 İstiklal Caddesi
MAP J6–L4

Packed with shoppers by day, Beyoğlu's main street *(see p86)* is also an entertainment hub by night and home to several interesting sights. It is pedestrianized, but you can hop on the tram, which runs the street's entire length. Be aware that many protests and demonstrations take place here. Visitors are advised to stay well away from them.

4 Mevlevi Monastery
(Mevlevi Tekkesi)

MAP J6 ▪ Galip Dede Cad 15
▪ (0212) 245 41 41 ▪ Open 9am–4pm
Wed–Mon ▪ Adm; book in advance
for dancing

This late 18th-century lodge
belonged to a Sufi sect of Islamic
mystics and is now the Whirling
Dervish Museum (Mevlevihane
Müzesi). Sufi Whirling Dervishes
still dance here on Sundays; look
out for times on a board outside.
The museum contains many
artifacts associated with dervish
rituals, such as begging bowls and
musical instruments, but star of the
show is the beautiful *semahane*, or
ritual dance hall, upstairs.

5 Military Museum
(Askeri Müze)

MAP B4 ▪ Vali Konağı Cad, Harbiye
▪ (0212) 233 27 20 ▪ Open 9am–5pm
Wed–Sun (Mehter Band 3pm daily)
▪ Adm charge

Housed in the former military
academy where Atatürk was
educated, the museum contains
thousands of exhibits telling the
story of warfare from Ottoman times
to World War II. Chain mail, armour,
swords and embroidered tents are
on display; one room is devoted to
Atatürk's career. A highlight is the
show by the Mehter Band, recreating
the military music of the Janissaries,
the elite Ottoman corps.

6 Taksim Square
(Taksim Meydanı)

MAP L4

The busy hub of modern
Beyoğlu, Taksim Square was
the end of the water supply
line laid down by Mahmut
I in 1732 – his original stone
reservoir still stands at
the square's western end.
On the same side of the
square is the Monument
of Independence, a
patriotic sculpture
of Atatürk and other
revolutionary heroes
erected in 1928.

**Monument of
Independence**

MILITARY MARCHES

The Mehter music performed daily
in the grounds of the Military Museum
has been widely influential. Founded
in the 14th century during the reign
of Osman I, the Ottoman Janissary
bands accompanied the army as it
marched to war, intimidating the
enemy through the sheer volume of
their huge drums, cymbals and *zurnas*
(traditional reed instruments). The
rousing military style of Mehter music
strongly influenced the compositions
of Beethoven and Mozart, as well
as the da Souza military marches
played by today's brass bands.

7 Museum of Innocence
(Masümiyet Müzesi)

MAP K6 ▪ Dalgıç Cıkmaz 2,
Çukurcuma ▪ (0212) 252 97 38
▪ Open 10am–6pm Tue–Sun
(until 9pm Thu) ▪ Adm ▪ www.
masumiyetmuzesi.myshopio.com

Nobel-prize-winning Turkish author
Orhan Pamuk's book *The Museum of
Innocence* is the inspiration for this
museum. The thousands of cigarette
butts that the angst-ridden protago-
nist of the novel smoked are on
display, along with other ephemera,
in a converted period town house.

8 Çukurcuma

MAP K5

The old quarter of Beyoğlu is today a
centre for second-hand and
antiques trades. Its mansions
and warehouses have been
restored, and this is now a
great place to browse for anything from antique cabinets to
modern upholstery materials
or 1960s comics.

9 Church of SS
Peter and Paul
(Sen Piyer Kilisesi)

MAP F3 ▪ Galata Kulesi
Sok 44, Karaköy ▪ (0212)
249 23 85 ▪ Open
10:30am–noon Sun

When their original
church was requisi-
tioned as a mosque in

the early 16th century, the Dominican brothers of Galata moved to this site, just below the Galata Tower. The church was built in the style of a basilica with four side-altars. It also has a blue cupola studded with gold stars over the choir. Mass is said here in Italian every morning. Ring the bell by the tiny door (accessed through the courtyard) to gain admittance.

The Tortoise Trainer, **Pera Museum**

🔟 Pera Museum
(Pera Müzesi)

MAP J5 ■ Meşrutiyet Cad 65 ■ (0212) 334 99 00 ■ Open 10am–7pm Tue–Sat (until 10pm Fri), noon–6pm Sun ■ Adm ■ www.peramuseum.com

The old Bristol Hotel has been revived as the home of this museum and gallery (see p44), privately run by the Suna and İnan Kıraç Foundation set up by wealthy Turkish industrialists. The first two floors display the Kıraç family's collections of Kutahya tiles and ceramics and Anatolian weights and measures. The next floor has an intriguing collection, most of it by European artists, detailing life at the Ottoman imperial court from the 17th century onwards. The top storeys are given over to temporary shows.

A DAY IN BEYOĞLU

Military Museum 1.2 km (1 mile) · Taksim Square
Nevizade Sokak
Church of St Anthony of Padua · Galatasaray High School · Galatasaray Baths
İstiklal Caddesi · Çukurcuma
Beyoğlu İş Merkezi
Asmalı Mescit Sokağı · Church of St Mary Draperis
Mevlevi Monastery
Galata Tower · Galip Dede Caddesi

▶ MORNING

Walk over the Galata Bridge and head up to the **Galata Tower** (see p82). Take the lift to the top to walk the perimeter balcony and enjoy the breathtaking view. Back at the bottom, refresh yourself at a traditional tea garden before taking a leisurely stroll up **Galip Dede Caddesi** (see p87) to peer into the music shops and have a go on a traditional Turkish instrument if the fancy takes you. Continue on towards Tünel (see p86) and learn about the Whirling dervishes at the **Mevlevi Monastery**. For lunch, try a small street café on bohemian **Asmalı Mescit Sokağı**, or go Gallic on Fransız Sokağı (French Street).

AFTERNOON

Walk up İstiklal Caddesi (see p86) browsing the music shops, fashion stores and **Beyoğlu İş Merkezi** (see p87), then visit the **Church of St Mary Draperis** and the **Church of Saint Anthony of Padua** (see p86). Get to the **Military Museum** in time for the 3pm performance by the Mehter Band. Head to **Çukurcuma** via Taksim Square, stopping off for some refreshments if you need to. After browsing the vast array of antique shops in Çukurcuma, relax at the **Galatasaray Baths** (see p86). Refreshed, wander past the **Galatasaray High School** (see p86) and cut through to boisterous **Nevizade Sokak** (see p89) to choose a place to wine and dine. Fish is the speciality here – start with a few *meze* then try the catch of the day, washing it down with a glass of *rakı*.

See map on p83 ←

İstiklal Caddesi

1 Tünel
MAP J6

The 573-m (1,880-ft) Tünel is a funicular that runs up the steep slope from Galata Bridge to Beyoğlu. Built by the French in 1874, it is one of the world's oldest metros.

2 Christ Church
MAP J6 ■ Serdar Ekrem Sok 52 ■ (0212) 251 56 16

The centre of the Anglican community in Istanbul, this church was consecrated in 1868 as the Crimean Memorial Church, using English money and Maltese stone.

Galatasaray Baths

3 Galatasaray Baths (Tarihi Galatasaray Hamamı)
MAP K5 ■ Turnacıbaşı Sok 24 (off İstiklal Cad) ■ (0212) 252 42 42 (men) & (0212) 249 43 42 (women) ■ Open 7am–10pm (men), 8am–9pm (women) daily ■ Adm charge

Wealthy Istanbulites come here to be sweated, scrubbed and scraped in one of the finest *hamams* in Istanbul, built by Beyazıt II in 1481. Today the baths are fully modernized but still retain their charm. Men and women bathe separately.

4 Church of St Anthony of Padua
MAP J5 ■ İstiklal Cad 171 ■ (0212) 244 09 35 ■ Open 8am–7:30pm daily (closed 12:30–3pm Sun)

This red-brick Neo-Gothic building is the largest working Catholic church in the city. The church was built in 1911 by Istanbul-born Italian architect Giulio Mongeri.

5 Swedish Consulate
MAP J6 ■ İstiklal Cad 497 ■ (0212) 334 06 00 ■ Open for events only

Built in 1757, this magnificent embassy was reconstructed after a fire in 1870.

6 Yapı Kredi Vedat Nedim Tör Müzesi
MAP J5 ■ İstiklal Cad 285 ■ (0212) 252 47 00 ■ Open 10am–6:45pm Mon–Fri, 10am–5:45pm Sat, 1–5:45pm Sun

This smart art gallery was set up by one of Turkey's largest banks.

7 Galatasaray High School (Galatasaray Lisesi)
MAP K5 ■ İstiklal Cad 159 ■ (0212) 249 11 00 ■ Closed to the public

Originally founded by Sultan Beyazıt II in 1481 to train imperial pages, this is still Turkey's premier school.

8 Fish Market (Balık Pazarı)
MAP J5

A fish, fruit and veg market by day, by night the adjacent alleys are filled with cheap and lively restaurants.

9 Flower Arcade (Çiçek Pasajı)
MAP K4

Housed in the Cité de Pera (1876), one of several ornate Victorian arcades along İstiklal, this former flower market is now an entertaining (if touristy) tavern quarter.

10 Nostalgic Tram
MAP J5–L4

The horse-drawn tram service that rumbled along İstiklal Caddesi in the 19th century was electrified in 1914 (the horses were taken off to war). The service closed in 1961, but was revived in 1990. Its red carriages have become an icon of Beyoğlu. Buy tickets at either end of the line.

Places to Shop

1 Aznavur Pasajı
MAP K5 ■ İstiklal Cad 108, Galatasaray Meydanı

This Italian-style arcade has been on İstiklal Caddesi since 1883. You can buy a range of handmade goods here, including jewellery, clothes and souvenirs, on any of the nine floors.

2 Galip Dede Caddesi
MAP J6 ■ Tünel

Musical instruments, such as the traditional *oud*, handmade violins and locally made cymbals, are sold at a string of specialist music shops in this small street.

3 Çukurcuma
MAP K5

The streets between Cihangir and Galatasaray form part of the old quarter and are the best spots for antique-hunting *(see p84)*.

4 Avrupa Pasajı
MAP J5 ■ Meşrutiyet Cad 16

The 22 shops in this quiet, attractive old arcade carry a fine selection of jewellery, ceramics and other traditional Turkish crafts. There are also quirkier souvenirs such as old prints and maps.

5 Beyoğlu İş Merkezi
MAP J5 ■ İstiklal Cad 187

A haven for bargain-hunters, the three-storey Beyoğlu İş Merkezi is filled with tiny shops selling mainly high-street fashion labels. Many of the products here are second-hand or surplus; hence the rock-bottom prices. A tailor's shop in the basement can make alterations on the same day.

6 Koton
MAP K4 ■ İstiklal Cad 54 in Demirören AVM

You'll find both men's and women's fashions at this reasonably priced Turkish chain store. Designs are updated regularly and include party- and daywear.

Interior of Homer Books

7 Homer Books
MAP K5 ■ Yeni Çarşı Cad 12/A, Beyoğlu

One of the best-stocked bookshops in the city, Homer Books has English-language titles on all matters Turkey and Istanbul. Staff here are English-speaking too.

8 Mavi Jeans
MAP K5 ■ İstiklal Cad 117

Jeans made from organic cotton and hip Istanbul T-shirts are among the stylish items available from one of Turkey's most popular fashion brands.

9 By Retro
MAP F2 ■ Suriye Pasajı 166/C

Set at the end of the historic Syria Passage arcade, this store sells vintage clothing and other interesting retro goods.

10 Ali Muhiddin Hacı Bekir
MAP K4 ■ İstiklal Cad 83A

The place for *lokum* (Turkish delight), this is the Beyoğlu branch of the confectioners who invented the stuff in 1777. Other treats include *akide* (boiled sweets), *helva* and baklava.

***Lokum* at Ali Muhiddin Hacı Bekir**

See map on p83

Nightlife

Performance at Nardis Jazz Club

① Nardis Jazz Club
MAP F3 ■ Kuledibi Sok 14
■ (0212) 244 63 27

There's live music every night. Find a table near the stage and choose from the menu of salads and pasta.

② Babylon
Bomontii Bira Fabrikası 1, Şişli ■ (0212) 334 01 90 ■ www. babylon.com.tr

Housed in a converted brewery north of Taksim Square, Babylon is indisputably the city's best venue for live music of every kind, especially alternative foreign and Turkish bands.

③ Mektup
MAP K5 ■ Iman Adnan Sok 20, off İstiklal Caddesi ■ (0212) 251 01 10

One of the best places in Beyoğlu to listen to Turkish folk music and have a glass of beer.

④ Jolly Joker
MAP K5 ■ Balans Balo Sok 22
■ (0212) 251 70 20

Micro-brewery and live music venue combined, this is the place to come to see mainstream contemporary Turkish music acts.

⑤ Süheyla
MAP J4 ■ Kalyoncu Kulluk Cad 19 (behind Balık Pazarı)
■ (0212) 251 83 47

Süheyla is one of the best places to hear *fasıl* – the music of the *meyhanes* (*see p110*). The set menu includes unlimited *rakı*.

⑥ Minimuzikhol
MAP L5 ■ Soğancı Sok 7, off Sıraselviler Cad ■ (0212) 245 19 96

Small, lively club attracting discerning clubbers who come for the techno, dubstep and hip-hop. Attracts internationally acclaimed DJs on occasion.

⑦ Garaj Istanbul
MAP K5 ■ Kaymakam Reşat Bey Sok 11A, off Yeni Çarşı Cad ■ (0212) 244 44 99

Tucked away in a Beyoğlu backstreet, this club offers an adventurous programme of theatre performances, live bands and other cultural events.

⑧ 360
MAP J5 ■ İstikal Cad 163
■ (0212) 251 10 42

People flock to this rooftop terrace with superb views. The club offers lounge music with dinner, and a resident DJ for a funkier dance sound after midnight.

Outdoor seating on terrace at 360

⑨ Peyote
MAP J4 ■ Kameriye Sok 4, off Hamalbaşı Cad ■ (0212) 251 43 98

This popular local venue for alternative and world-music bands draws a young crowd with its low prices and up-and-coming acts.

⑩ Salon İKSV
MAP J6 ■ Sadi Konuralp Cad 5, off Refik Saydam Cad
■ (0212) 334 07 00

An intimate venue for classical, jazz, world music, plus dance and theatre.

Bars, Cafés and Restaurants

① Galata House
MAP F2 ■ Galata Kulesi
Sok 15 ■ (0212) 245 18 61
■ Closed Mon ■ ₺₺

Galata House is a true original –
a restaurant in a converted British
jail. It serves delicious Russian-
Georgian-Turkish food.

Elegant seating area at Galata House

② İmroz
MAP K4 ■ Nevizade Sokak
24, Beyoğlu ■ (0212) 249 90 73 ■ ₺₺

Of the several fish restaurants on
the tiny street of Nevizade Sokak,
this (see p50) may be the best.

③ Kafe Ara
MAP J5 ■ Tosbağa Sok 8, off
Yeni Çarşı Cad ■ (0212) 245 41 05 ■ ₺₺

There's an intellectual, artistic vibe
at this café serving fresh, light food
(but no alcohol). It is decorated with
the work of Turkey's most famous
photographer, Ara Güler.

④ Refik
MAP J6 ■ Sofyali Sok 6–8
■ (0212) 243 28 34 ■ ₺₺

A true meyhane with meze,
free-flowing wine and a bohemian
clientele, Refik is stuck in the
past and all the better for it.

⑤ Mikla
MAP J5 ■ The Marmara Pera,
Meşrutiyet Cad 15, Beyoğlu
■ (0212) 293 56 56 ■ ₺₺

Mediterranean and Scandanavian
flavours are fused at this cool
rooftop restaurant. The food
and views are sublime.

PRICE CATEGORIES

For a typical meal of meze and main
course for one without alcohol, and
including taxes and extra charges.

₺ under ₺70 ₺₺ ₺70–120
₺₺₺ over ₺120

⑥ Mandabatmaz
MAP J5 ■ Olivia Geçidi,
off İstiklal Cad ■ ₺

Sit on low stools in this hole-in-the-
wall café to drink Istanbul's very
best, rich and aromatic Turkish
coffee at a bargain price.

⑦ Leb-i-Derya
MAP J6 ■ Kumbaracı Yokuşu
57/6 ■ (0212) 293 49 89 ■ ₺₺

Start with a cocktail, then sample
their speciality, the 40-spiced steak
Mahmudiye. Come early if you want
to eat on the tiny roof terrace. Reservations essential at weekends.

⑧ Yeni Lokanta
MAP J6 ■ Kumbaracı Yokuşu
66, Beyoğlu ■ (0212) 292 25 50 ■ ₺₺₺

Top-notch place (see p50) serving
traditional Turkish dishes with a
contemporary flavour.

⑨ Sensus
MAP F2 ■ Büyük Hendek Cad
5, Galata ■ (0212) 245 56 57 ■ ₺₺

This trendy basement wine bar
stocks dozens of different Turkish
wines and a range of cheeses to go
with them. Packed weekend nights.

⑩ Meze by Lemon Tree
MAP J6 ■ Meşrutiyet Cad
83/B, Beyoğlu
■ (0212) 252
83 02 ■ ₺₺₺

The traditional
Turkish meyhane
is given a con-
temporary
makeover in this
stylish restaurant.

**Hummus, Meze
by Lemon Tree**

The meze here are superb. Book well
in advance for weekend evenings.

See map on p83 ←

🔟 The Bosphorus

Sultan's throne, Naval Museum

The Bosphorus is one of the world's busiest waterways, part of the only shipping lane from the Black Sea to the Mediterranean. Just 32-km (20-miles) long and varying in width from 3.5 km (about 2.2 miles) to 698 m (2,290 ft), it connects the Black Sea to the Sea of Marmara, dividing Europe from Asia. The straits are governed by international maritime law, so Turkey has authority only over vessels flying a Turkish flag. Navigation can be difficult, since the mixture of fresh water from the Black Sea and salt water from the Sea of Marmara creates complex cross-currents. All of this is fascinating, but to most of us what really counts is the beauty of the waterway and the historic buildings that line its shores.

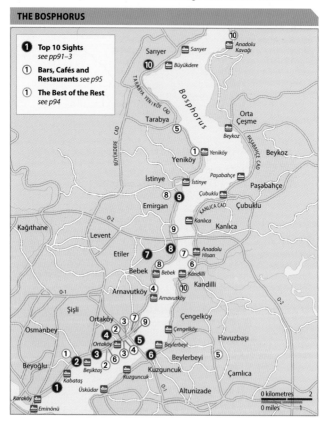

THE BOSPHORUS

① Top 10 Sights
see pp91–3

① Bars, Cafés and Restaurants *see p95*

① The Best of the Rest
see p94

An exhibit at the Istanbul Modern gallery

1 Istanbul Modern
(İstanbul Modern)

MAP G2 ■ Meclis-i Mebusan Cad, Karaköy; temporary location: Meşrütiyet Cad 99, Beyoğlu ■ (0212) 334 73 00 ■ Open 10am–6pm Tue–Sun (until 8pm Thu) ■ Adm ■ www.istanbulmodern.org

This cutting-edge gallery's small collection of modern Turkish painting, sculpture and photography is augmented by touring exhibitions, video and audio installations, and an arthouse cinema (see p44). The gallery was shifted to a temporary location due to ongoing restoration and will shift back to its original location in 2020.

2 Dolmabahçe Palace
(Dolmabahçe Sarayı)

In 1856, Sultan Abdül Mecit removed his entire family and government from the Topkapı to this European-style palace at Beşiktaş on the Bosphorus shore.

3 Naval Museum
(Deniz Müzesi)

MAP C5 ■ Hayrettin Paşa İskelesi Sok, Beşiktaş ■ (0212) 327 43 45 ■ Tram Kabataş then 5-min walk ■ Open 9am–5pm Tue–Fri (summer: 10am–6pm Sat & Sun) ■ Adm

Ottoman Turkey's great maritime history is celebrated in this state-of-the-art museum splendidly situated right on the banks of the Bosphorus. Exhibits to look out for, on the main

floor, are lavishly adorned imperial caïques – high-prowed barges that were used for ferrying the royal family along the Bosphorus. The largest, built for Sultan Mehmet IV in 1648, was 40-m- (130-ft-) long and required 144 bostancıs (oarsmen) to row it. Beautifully carved figureheads of ships along with a chronological display of the Ottoman naval history are housed on the floor below.

4 Yıldız Palace
(Yıldız Sarayı)

MAP C4 ■ Yıldız Cad, Beşiktaş ■ (0212) 258 30 80 ■ Palace: open 9am–6pm Wed–Mon; park: open 10am–5:30pm daily (winter: until 4pm) ■ Adm for palace

Much of this rambling palace was built by Sultan Abdül Hamit II (ruled 1876–1909), a highly skilled carpenter whose former workshop now houses the Yıldız Palace Museum. The park and its pavilions are also open to the public. In the grounds is the Imperial Porcelain Factory, now mass-producing china where once they made fine porcelain.

Yıldız Palace in Beşiktaş

The soaring Bosphorus Bridge

5 Bosphorus Bridge
(Boğaziçi Köprüsü)

MAP C4

In 1973, to mark the 50th anniversary of the establishment of the Republic of Turkey, this soaring creation, linking Europe and Asia across the Bosphorus straits, was officially opened. At 1,560 m (5,120 ft) long, it is the world's sixth-longest suspension bridge. Pedestrians are not allowed onto the bridge, so if you want plenty of time to admire the view, cross at rush hour when the heavy traffic routinely becomes gridlocked.

6 Beylerbeyi Palace
(Beylerbeyi Sarayi)

MAP C5 ■ Çayırbaşı Cad (next to Bosphorus Bridge) ■ (0216) 321 93 20 ■ Bus 15 and 15B from Üsküdar ■ Guided tours: 9am–5pm Tue–Sun (Oct–Apr: until 4pm) ■ Adm

This small, frivolously ornate powder-puff of a palace was built in 1860–65 by Sultan Abdül Aziz as a summer retreat. It was here that Sultan Abdül Hamit II lived out his days in captivity after he was deposed in 1909. You will either be charmed or overwhelmed by the incredible detailing of architect Sarkis Balyan's Oriental Rococo style. Look for the inlaid stairs in the Fountain Room, the Bohemian crystal chandeliers, the hand-decorated doorknobs, the Hereke carpets and the walnut-and-rosewood furniture made by Abdül Hamit *(see p91)* himself.

7 Aşiyan Museum
(Aşiyan Müzesi)

MAP U2 ■ Aşiyan Yokuşu, Bebek ■ (0212) 263 69 86 ■ Open 9am–4:30pm Tue, Wed, Fri & Sat

The poet and utopian philosopher Tevfik Fikret (1867–1915), founder of the Edebiyat-i Cedid (New Literature) movement, built this wooden mansion, now on the campus of Boğaziçi University, in 1906. It recalls the movement with the personal belongings and photos of the members.

8 Fortress of Europe
(Rumeli Hisarı)

MAP U2 ■ Yahya Kemal Cad ■ (0212) 263 53 05 ■ Open 9am–4:30pm Thu–Tue ■ Adm

In 1452, as he prepared for his final attack on Constantinople, Mehmet II built this vast fortress at the narrowest point of the Bosphorus, opposite the earlier Fortress of Asia (Anadolu Hisarı) *(see p94)*, to cut the flow

PRINCELY PARANOIA

Terrified both of plots to seize his throne and of seaborne attack by foreign warships on Dolmabahçe Palace, Sultan Abdül Hamit II **(below)**, who ruled from 1876 to 1909, removed himself from the Dolmabahçe to live at the much smaller Yıldız Palace *(see p91)*, the core of which – the State Apartments (Büyük Mabeyn) – dates to the reign of Sultan Selim III (ruled 1789–1807). Abdül Hamit built a sprawling complex of pavilions and villas in the palace grounds, and he supposedly never spent two nights in the same bed. He was over-thrown in April 1909.

of supplies reaching the city. The castle's three main towers are surrounded by a huge curtain wall with 13 bastions. The main tower later became a prison.

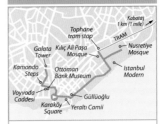

The verdant Fortress of Europe

⑨ Sakıp Sabancı Museum
(Sakıp Sabancı Müzesi)
MAP U2 ■ Sakıp Sabancı Cad 42, Emirgan ■ (0212) 277 22 00 ■ Open 10am–6pm Tue–Sun (until 8pm Wed) ■ Adm ■ www.sakipsabancimuzesi.org

The summer residence of the Sabancı family of industrialists from 1951 to 1999, the Atlı Köşk (Horse Mansion) is now a museum set in stunning gardens that overlook the Bosphorus. The exhibits here include calligraphy of the Ottoman era, and paintings by leading 19th- and 20th-century Turkish artists. The modern extension is a well-designed art gallery housing major touring exhibitions.

⑩ Sadberk Hanım Museum
(Sadberk Hanım Müzesi)
MAP U1 ■ Piyasa Cad 27–29, Büyükdere ■ (0212) 242 38 13 ■ Open 10am–5pm Thu–Tue ■ Adm ■ www.sadberkhanimmuzesi.org.tr

The Sadberk Hanım Museum boasts a must-see collection that includes a range of Turkish embroidery as well as Anatolian figurines, Assyrian cuneiform trade tablets, Hittite coins and gold jewellery.

Anatolian figurine

A WALK THROUGH KARAKÖY

▶ **MORNING**

Start your day at the Karaköy tram stop, then head uphill to the early 20th-century Minerva Han, adorned with cupid statues on its tiled façade. Turn left along Voyvoda Caddesi, named for Vlad the Impaler, whose decapitated head (it is said) was displayed here. If you have time, explore the **Ottoman Bank Museum** *(see p54)*, which houses the SALT Galata art gallery. The **Kamondo Steps** lead towards the Galata Tower. Walk back down along Karaköy Caddesi and turn right to visit **Yeraltı Camii** *(Kemkaneş Cad 23, Karaköy)*, an underground mosque built on the site of an old Byzantine tower.

AFTERNOON

Continue along Karaköy and turn left onto Rihtim Caddesi. The **Güllüoğlu** baklava shop here is the finest in Turkey; the Galata Rihtim Köftecisi nearby offers a healthier option for lunch. Follow the road round between two fine small mosques, the **Nusretiye Mosque** *(Meclis-ı Mebusan Caddesi, Tophane)* on the right, built by Kirkor Balyan in the 1820s, and the **Kılıç Ali Paşa Mosque** *(Kenmeraltı Cad 50, Karaköy)*, built by Sinan in 1580. Turn right onto the main road and, just after the Mimar Sinan University building, turn right again. Follow the signs through the old docks to **Istanbul Modern** *(see p91)*, where you can watch the sunset with a cocktail in the chic café-bar overlooking the Bosphorus. Then take the tram to Kabataş and the funicular up the hill to Taksim Square *(see p84)* for an evening meal.

See map on p90

The Best of the Rest

1 National Palaces Painting Museum
(Milli Saraylar Resim Müzesi)

MAP C5 ▪ Hayrettin Paşa Iskelesi Sok, Beşiktaş ▪ (0212) 261 42 98 ▪ Bus 25E, 28, 40, 56 ▪ Open 9am–5pm Tue, Wed, Fri–Sun

Fine art from the 19th and 20th centuries is displayed in this museum, in the Crown Princes' Suite at Dolmabahçe Palace.

2 Çırağan Palace
(Çırağan Sarayı)

MAP C5 ▪ Çırağan Cad 32, Beşiktaş ▪ (0212) 326 46 46 ▪ Bus 25E, 40 ▪ www.ciragan-palace.com

Sultan Abdül Aziz spent a fortune on this confection of a palace, built in 1874, before pronouncing it damp and moving out. The Palace is now home to a luxury hotel.

3 Ortaköy
MAP C4 ▪ Bus 25RE, 40

This pretty village beside the Bosphorus Bridge has many waterfront cafés, restaurants and clubs, and a weekend craft market.

4 Arnavutköy
MAP U3 ▪ Ferry or road

Once noted for its strawberries, the village of Arnavutköy is now better known for the charming *yalıs* (wooden mansions) that line its pretty waterfront.

Waterfront, Arnavutköy

5 SAV Automobile Museum
(SAV Otomobil Müzesi)

MAP V3 ▪ Bosna Bulvarı 104, Çengelköy (Asian side) ▪ (0216) 329 50 30 ▪ Open 11am–6pm Fri–Sun ▪ Adm

Here you will find Turkey's largest collection of antique cars.

6 Küçüksu Palace
(Küçüksu Kasrı)

MAP U3 ▪ Küçüksu Cad, Beykoz (Asian side) ▪ (0216) 332 33 03 ▪ Bus 15 from Üsküdar ▪ Open 9:30am–4pm Tue, Wed, Fri–Sun (guided tours only) ▪ Adm

Küçüksu, with two rivers known to the Ottomans as the "Sweet Waters of Asia", was a playground for the Imperial court. The palace was built as a lodge in 1857 for Abdül Mecit.

7 Fortress of Asia
(Anadolu Hisarı)

MAP U2 ▪ Boat or road to Kanlıca

Built by Beyazıt I in 1391, this fortress on the Asian side is a smaller counterpart to the Fortress of Europe, added by Mehmet II in 1452, directly across the Bosphorus (see pp90–3).

8 Emirgan Park
(Emirgan Parkı)

MAP U2 ▪ Emirgan Sahil Yolu ▪ Bus 25E, 40 ▪ Open 7am–10pm daily

This attractive park (see p47) with botanic planting is a venue for the Tulip Festival (see p56) each April.

9 Borusan Contemporary
MAP U2 ▪ Perili Köşk Baltalımanı Hısar Cad 5, Rumelihisarı ▪ (0212) 393 52 00 ▪ Bus 22, 40T ▪ Open 10am–8pm Sat & Sun ▪ Adm

A fashionable office block in the week, Istanbul's coolest gallery at weekends, with great Bosphorus views from the roof terrace.

10 Anadolu Kavağı
MAP V1 ▪ Asian side

This is the last stop for the Bosphorus ferry. Climb the hill to Yoros Castle, a ruined 14th-century Genoese fortress.

Bars, Cafés and Restaurants

PRICE CATEGORIES

For a typical meal of *meze* and main
course for one without alcohol, and
including taxes and extra charges.

₺ under ₺70 ₺₺ ₺70–120
₺₺₺ over ₺120

Lavish seating area at Laledan

1 Kaşıbeyaz
Köybaşı Cad 10, Sariyer
■ (0212) 299 50 00 ■ ₺₺

This upscale kebab restaurant offers
great views of the Bosphorus, good
food and great service.

2 Feriye Lokantası
MAP C4 ■ Çırağan Cad 40,
Ortaköy ■ (0212) 227 22 16/7 ■ ₺₺

Picturesquely situated on the Ortaköy
waterfront, the Feriye serves delicious
Ottoman dishes including charcoal-
grilled lamb. Book ahead.

3 The House Café
MAP C4 ■ Salhane Sok 1,
Ortaköy ■ (0212) 227 26 99 ■ Book
for brunch ■ ₺₺

The Ortaköy branch of this popular
café chain serves unusual pizzas
(such as pear, Roquefort and honey),
together with seafood, and brunch
staples. Its waterfront decking is a
draw during the summer months.

4 Anjelique
MAP C4 ■ Muallim Naci
Cad, Salhane Sok 5, Ortaköy
■ (0212) 327 28 44/5 ■ ₺₺

On the first-floor waterfront terrace
is the upmarket Da Mario Italian
restaurant (summer only), while
the second and third floors serve
international cuisine. The two upper
floors become a nightclub after the
dishes are cleared away.

5 Kıyı
MAP U2 ■ Kefeliköy Cad 126,
Tarabya ■ (0212) 262 00 02

A smart and stylish fish joint in the
posh suburb of Tarabya. The decor
is plain chic and the *meze* and fish
mains are cooked to perfection.

6 Laledan, Beşiktaş
MAP C5 ■ Çırağan Cad,
Beşiktaş ■ (0212) 236 73 33 ■ ₺₺₺

Part of the luxurious Çırağan
Palace Hotel Kempinski, the
Laledan restaurant serves great
brunches in a fairy-tale setting.

7 Supperclub
MAP C4 ■ Muallim Naci Cad
65, Ortaköy ■ (0212) 261 19 88

This trendy club on the Bosphorus
waterfront is an ambitious and
intriguing concept. There's a cool,
all-white interior, subtle electronic
sounds and plenty of lounging
sofas to chill out on.

8 Poseidon
MAP U3 ■ Çevdet Paşa
Cad 58 ■ (0212) 287 95 31 ■ ₺₺

Located in trendy Bebek, this
chic seafood restaurant offers
mouthwatering food.

9 Blackk
MAP U3 ■ Muallim Naci Cad 1,
Kuruçeşme ■ (0212) 236 72 78

DJ-led international pop, R&B
and other musical styles keep
patrons entertained at this night
club set by the Bosphorus.

10 Suna'nın Yeri
MAP U3 ■ İskele Cad 2/A,
Kandilli ■ (0216) 332 32 41 ■ ₺₺

A well-established and unpretentious
fish joint by the ferry dock in the
Asian suburb of Kandilli. The food
here is a fraction of the price of
most Bosphorus fish restaurants,
and just as good.

See map on p90

🔟 Asian Istanbul and Princes' Islands

Asian Istanbul is just a 20-minute ferry ride across the Bosphorus or one metro stop through the Bosphorus tunnel. Üsküdar is home to some venerable Ottoman mosques and the quirky off-shore Leander's Tower. To the south, Kadıköy is more lively than conservative Üsküdar, with plenty of bars. Between these two suburbs are the Florence Nightingale Museum and German-built Haydarpaşa Station. The Princes' Islands are easily reached by ferry from Kabataş. Places of exile in the Byzantine era, summer retreats for minority Jewish and Christian groups in the 19th century, today they are traffic-free and an ideal place to swim, cycle or just relax at a harbour front restaurant.

ASIAN ISTANBUL AND PRINCES' ISLANDS

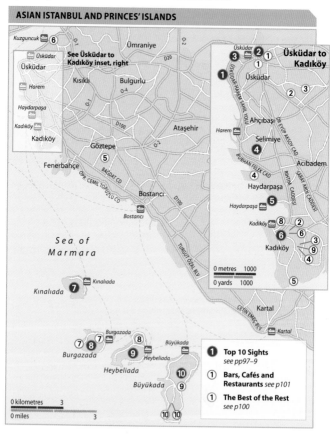

The picturesque Leander's Tower

1 Leander's Tower
(Kız Kulesi)

MAP W3 ■ (0216) 342 47 47
■ Tower: open 12:30–6:30pm
Mon–Fri, 9:15am–6:30pm Sat
& Sun; restaurant: open until 1am

According to Greek myth, Leander drowned while trying to swim the Dardanelles from his home town of Abydos on the Asian side to meet his lover Hero, a priestess in Sestos on the other shore. He is commemorated in the English name for this 18th-century tower on an islet offshore from Üsküdar. Its Turkish name means "Maiden's Tower", in reference to a legendary Byzantine princess who was told that she would die of a snakebite and was locked up on the island for her own protection, only for a snake to arrive in a basket of figs. In its time, the tower has served as a quarantine centre and a customs office; nowadays, it houses a restaurant. It had a cameo role in the 1999 James Bond film *The World Is Not Enough*.

The Lady with the Lamp, 1891

2 İskele Mosque
(İskele Camii)

MAP X2 ■ Kurşunlu Medrese Sok
■ (0216) 321 93 20 ■ Ferry Üsküdar
or Marmaray ■ Open daily (closed
at prayer times)

This beautiful mosque, officially called the Mihrimah Sultan Mosque, was a present, built in 1547–8, from Süleyman I to his favourite daughter, Mihrimah. Its raised portico offers fine views down to the main square.

3 Şemsi Paşa Mosque
(Şemsi Paşa Camii)

MAP W2 ■ Sahil Yolu
■ Ferry Üsküdar or
Marmaray metro
■ Open daily

Legend has it that birds will not land on or dirty this mosque out of respect for its beauty and the reputation of its architect. It is one of Mimar Sinan's last works (see p27), built in 1580 for Şemsi Ahmet Paşa, Grand Vizier to Süleyman I. Made of white stone, it is very modest in size and sits in a picturesque location among the waterfront fish restaurants.

4 Florence Nightingale Museum

MAP X5 ■ Selimiye Kışlası, Çeşme-i-
Kebir Cad ■ (0216) 556 81 66 ■ Ferry
to Harem ■ Open 9am–5pm Mon–Fri
■ Visitors should fax (0216) 553 10 09
requesting permission to visit, at
least 2 days in advance, giving names,
nationalities, passport details and
contact number

In the northwest tower of the Selimiye Barracks is a moving tribute to the formidable Florence Nightingale (1820–1910), who in 1854 gathered a group of 38 women and set up a hospital in Istanbul to nurse thousands of Turkish and allied soldiers wounded during the Crimean War – inventing modern nursing practice along the way. The museum contains her photographs and medallions, gifts from Sultan Abdül Mecit, and the lamp from which she got her nick-name, "the Lady of the Lamp". The vast barracks in which the museum is situated were begun in 1828 by Mahmut II to replace an earlier military building constucted by Selim III.

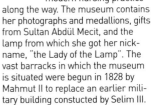

Interior of Haydarpaşa Station

5 Haydarpaşa Station
MAP C6 ◼ Haydarpaşa
İstasyon Cad ◼ **(0216) 336 04 75**
◼ **Ferry to Kadıköy**

Haydarpaşa Station is the largest station in Turkey and the most westerly train stop in Asia. It was completed in 1908 by German architects Otto Ritter and Helmuth Cuno, a gift from the German government of Kaiser Wilhelm II. Until recently, the station was the departure point for travellers heading further into Anatolia. The station remained dormant for a few years when a high speed line opened between Istanbul and Ankara, but it is likely that it will once again become Asian Istanbul's major rail terminus in 2020.

6 Kadıköy
MAP C6 ◼ **Frequent ferries from Eminönü and Karaköy**

Kadıköy, first settled as long ago as the Neolithic era, was the site of the Greek colony of Chalcedon, founded in 676 BC, nine years before the establishment of Byzantion *(see p60)*. However, Chalcedon proved to be more vulnerable to invaders than Byzantion, and it failed to flourish. Today, Kadıköy is a popular and attractive shopping area, but it has maintained its cosy, neighbourhood feel. The lively market area by the docks has fresh fruit and vegetables galore and is a good place to stock up on provisions. A nostalgic tram rumbles through the area down to fashionable Moda, in Asian Istanbul, where you can enjoy a pleasant stroll along the seafront. Fenerbahçe – one of Turkey's top football clubs – has its grounds, Şükrü Saraçoğlu Stadium, close by, so watch out for traffic jams on match days.

7 Kınalıada
MAP V6 ◼ **Ferry from Eminönü**

"Henna Island", Kınalıada is the nearest island to the city and yet the least visited. It has some reasonable beaches, and is popular in summer with Istanbul's dwindling Armenian community, which has a pretty church just above the village.

The main settlement on Kınalıada

8 Burgazada
MAP U6 ◼ **Ferry from Eminönü**

Beyond Kınalıada, the attractive little island of Burgazada is topped by a badly ruined Byzantine monastery. Of interest here is the museum of bohemian Turkish writer Sait Faik, which occupies a delightful period house *(see p100)*. Aside from this, visitors usually content themselves with a horse and carriage ride, a splash in the sea, or a fish meal along the waterfront.

Taking a ride on Heybeliada

9 Heybeliada
MAP V6 ■ Ferry from Eminönü

"Saddlebag Island" is so called as the island comprises two green hills, with a saddle between them. The third island in the chain, it's an ideal place to hire a bike and cycle around or ride on a horse-drawn carriage. The Greek Orthodox Haghia Triada seminary (see p100) dominates one hilltop. There are several pay beaches dotted around the island.

10 Büyükada
MAP V6 ■ Ferry from Eminönü

"Big Island" is, unsurprisingly, the largest of the islands, and the furthest from Istanbul. Horse and carriage rides are big here, as is the steep walk up to the Monastery of St George (see p100) and the next-door restaurant – both with fine sea views. Hire a bike and cycle to the Museum of the Princes' Islands (see p100).

LINKING EUROPE AND ASIA

The first bridge across the Bosphorus strait was built by the Persian Darius in 513 BC. After almost 2,500 years this was surpassed with the opening of the first Bosphorus suspension bridge in 1973. A second followed higher up the strait in 1988. In 2013, a section of one of Turkey's most significant infrastructure projects went into service when the tunnel from Sirkeci to Üsküdar opened. The Marmaray tunnel is the central point of the railway, running from Halkalı on the European side to Gebze on the Asian side. A third Bosphorus bridge was completed in 2016.

A DAY IN ASIA

▶ MORNING

Take the tram to Kabataş. Make sure you have your Istanbulkart or buy a handful of tokens at the ferry terminal. Pick up a timetable for ferry times. Summer weekends are very crowded aboard, so arrive early to bag a seat on a ferry to **Kınalıada** (the journey takes around 50 minutes). Visit the small **Armenian chapel** (Akgunluk Sokakı Kınalıada) on a hill just above Kınalıada's main settlement before catching another ferry south to **Burgazada**. Either hire a bike or horse-drawn carriage (fayton in Turkish) and head around the coast to **Kalpazankaya** (see p101) to enjoy a fine fish meal at the well-regarded restaurant here. It overlooks a small beach where you can swim in season.

AFTERNOON

Ride the ferry onto **Heybeliada** and explore the harbour front area. Look out for the **Aya Nikola** (Imralı So 11, Heybeliada) Greek Orthodox Church and have a Turkish coffee on the seafront while waiting for a ferry onto **Büyükada**. To find out about the history of these islands, either hire a bike or fayton and head for the **Museum of the Princes' Islands** (see p100) on Büyükada's east coast. The best (albeit stony) beach is Halik Köyü, on the west coast. Alternatively explore the fin de siècle mansions (Trotsky lived in one from 1929 to 1933) dotted around the town, or walk up to the **Monastery of St George** (see p100). The sea bus back to Kabataş takes half an hour; ferries, over an hour.

See map on p96 ←

The Best of the Rest

1 Yeni Valide Mosque
(Yeni Valide Camii)
MAP X2 ■ Hakimiyeti Milliye Cad ■ Ferry Üsküdar or Marmaray ■ Open prayer times only

This imposing mosque was built in 1710 by Ahmet III for his mother, Gülnuş Emetullah.

2 Atik Valide Mosque
(Atik Valide Camii)
MAP Y3 ■ Çinili Cami Sok ■ Bus 12C from Üsküdar ■ Open prayer times only

The huge complex of this mosque (see p40) was completed in 1583 for Nurbanu Valide Sultan, the Venetian-born Jewish wife of Selim II.

3 Tiled Mosque
(Çinili Camii)
MAP C5 ■ Çinili Hamam Sok 1, Üsküdar ■ Ferry or Marmaray to Üsküdar, then 20-min walk ■ Open prayer times only

Don't miss the İznik tiles inside this mosque, built in 1640.

4 British Crimean War Cemetery
MAP C6 ■ Off Burhan Felek Cad ■ Ferry Harem then 15-min walk

Most of the 6,000 Crimean War soldiers in this cemetery died of cholera rather than in battle. The War Memorial was erected in 1857.

5 Istanbul Toy Museum
(Istanbul Oyuncak Müzesi)
MAP U4 ■ Ömerpaşa Cad, Dr Zeki Zeren Sok 17, Göztepe ■ (0216) 359 45 50/1 ■ Open 9:30am–6pm Tue–Sun ■ Adm

Highlights of this collection of toys and miniatures from around the world include a French miniature violin from 1817 and a US doll from the 1820s.

6 Kuzguncuk
MAP C5

Wander through the streets in this old Jewish quarter, then stop for refreshment in one of the many eateries on the main street, İcadiye Caddesi.

7 Sait Faik Museum
(Sait Faik Müzesi)
MAP U6 ■ Cayiri Sok 15, Burgazada ■ Open 10am–noon & 2–5pm Tue–Sun, 10am–noon Sat

Turkish writer Sait Faik lived in this beautifully preserved home.

8 Haghia Triada Monastery
(Aya Triada Manastırı)
MAP V6 ■ Aya Triada Manastiriş, Heybeliada ■ (0216) 351 85 63

The Turkish authorities controversially closed the seminary here in the 1970s. Today it still functions as a monastery, but you need to book to gain entry.

9 Museum of the Princes' Islands
(Adalar Müzesi)
MAP V6 ■ Aya Nikola Mevkii, Büyükada ■ (0216) 382 64 30 ■ Open summer: 9am–6pm Tue–Sun (winter: until 5pm) ■ Adm

The focus here is on photographs of the Christian communities who lived here in the 19th century.

10 Monastery of St George
(Aya Yorgi Manastır)
MAP V6 ■ Yuca Tepe, Büyükada ■ Open 9am–6pm daily

Set on a hill, this working Orthodox monastery dates to the 12th century.

Monastery of St George

Bars, Cafés and Restaurants

PRICE CATEGORIES

For a typical meal of *meze* and main course for one without alcohol, and including taxes and extra charges.

....

₺ under ₺70 ₺₺ ₺70–120
₺₺₺ over ₺120

1 Kanaat, Üsküdar
MAP X2 ■ Selmanipak Cad 9
■ (0216) 553 37 91 ■ ₺

This traditional *lokanta* is as popular today as when it opened in 1933. It offers inexpensive and excellent Turkish food, as well as deliciously tempting puddings.

2 Otantik Anadolu Yemekleri, Kadıköy
MAP C6 ■ Muvakkithane Cad 62–4
■ (0216) 330 71 44 ■ ₺

Otantik offers hearty Anatolian cuisine with *gözleme* (stuffed crepes), fresh chicken, lamb casseroles and stuffed cabbage leaves.

3 Kadife Sokak, Kadıköy
MAP C6

Known to locals simply as Barlar Sokak ("Bar Street"), this lane is bursting with bars, cafés and clubs catering mainly to the young. Listen to avant-garde jazz or electronica in Karga (No. 16), taste fine wines in the garden at Isis (No. 26), or sit back and chill in Arka Oda (No. 18).

4 Buddha Rock Bar, Kadıköy
MAP U5 ■ Caferağa Mah, Kadife Sok 14 ■ (0216) 345 87 98 ■ ₺

This is a popular student bar, offering a range of cheap drinks, an energetic crowd, and live rock and blues alternating with a DJ.

5 Tarihi Moda İskelesi, Moda
MAP U4 ■ At the far end of the pier, off Moda İskele Cad ■ ₺₺

In an ornate little building on the old quayside, this café serves decent food and is a perfect spot for lunch.

Interior of Çiya restaurant

6 Çiya, Kadıköy
MAP C6 ■ Caferağa Mah, Guneşlibahçe Sok 44 ■ (0216) 418 51 15 ■ ₺₺

The kebabs in this informal gourmet restaurant are wonderful – the salads and *meze* are worth a look, too. There's a nice roof terrace.

7 Kalpazankaya, Burgazada
MAP U6 ■ Kalpazankaya Mevkii
■ (0216) 381 11 11 ■ ₺₺

A relaxed place on Burgazada's west shore with hot and cold *meze* and delicious grilled fish.

8 Deniz Yıldızı, Kadıköy
MAP U5 ■ İskele Cad, Eski Kadıköy İskelesi ■ (0216) 349 95 17 ■ ₺₺

Watch the boats from this old restaurant-bar on the seafront. It is open all day serving sandwiches, salads, beer, coffee and a full restaurant menu.

9 Viktor Levi, Kadıköy
MAP C6 ■ Moda Cad, Damacı Sok 4, Kadıköy ■ (0216) 449 93 29 ■ ₺₺

Popular wine bar in the heart of Kadıköy, with a delightful garden. Offers a wide range of sumptuous meals for lunch and dinner.

10 Kır Gazinosu, Büyükada
MAP V6 ■ Kır Gazinosu, Aya Yorgi, Yüce Tepe ■ ₺₺

Next to the Monastery of St George on Yüce Tepe hill, this casual place serves excellent starters, savoury pastries, chips and grills.

See map on p96

Streetsmart

A nostalgic tram at night on Istiklal
Caddesi, Taksim square

Getting To and Around Istanbul

Arriving by Air

Istanbul has two main airports, **Istanbul Airport** and **Sabiha Gökçen**. Flight times are 3.5 hours from London and 9 hours from New York.

Istanbul Airport, which opened in 2019 to replace Atatürk International, is located on the European side of the city, around 40 km (25 miles) north-west of the centre. IETT public buses run regularly to the city centre, as do the more comfortable and direct private Istanbul Otobüs A.Ş. vehicles. The best service is provided by **HAVAIST**, which runs to Yenikapı in the Old City and Taksim (for Beyoğlu and Galata). The journey time is around 1.5 hours for all services.

The smaller Sabiha Gökçen airport is used mainly by European budget carriers, such as easyJet, and is located on the Asian side of Istanbul, some 50 km (30 miles) from the city centre. **Havabüs** shuttle buses run to Taksim Square half-hourly between 4am and 1am, taking a minimum of 1 hour. A taxi will cost around ₺150.

Arriving by Coach

Turkish-operated coaches arrive from several cities in Europe, including Berlin, Prague, Vienna and Sofia. For services from London contact **Eurolines**. Istanbul's main coach station is **Esenler**, 10 km (6 miles) northwest of the city centre, where services from Europe

terminate. Esenler is also the main terminus for domestic services, though some stop at **Harem**, on the Asian shore. Many bus companies offer courtesy buses into the city centre; an alternative is the M1 metro.

Arriving by Rail

Owing to huge transport infrastructure projects in Istanbul, reaching the city by train from Europe is difficult. The best route from the UK to Istanbul is via either Bucharest or Belgrade and Sofia. Trains terminate at Halkalı, 25 km (15 miles) short of central Istanbul. Continue by Marmaray metro to the Sirkeci stop for the Old City. Get off at Yenikapı and transfer to the M2 metro for Beyoğlu/Karaköy. Websites such as **Man in Seat 61** are useful for booking train seats across Europe.

Arriving by Sea

Istanbul is a major cruise ship destination, with ships docking at the confluence of the Golden Horn and Bosphorus right in the heart of the city.

Travelling by Metro and Tram

The most convenient and cheapest way to travel around the city is by a combination of metro and tram, especially if you use an **Istanbulkart**. Both systems are operated by **Metro İstanbul** and run between 6am and midnight, but can be crowded during peak periods.

The M1 line links the ferry terminal at Yenikapı with the coach station at Esenler, and the M2 line the Old City with Galata, Beyoğlu and Taksim via a bridge across the Golden Horn. The Marmaray line runs west from Sirkeci to Kazlıçesme, on the line of the Theodosian Walls, and east under the Bosphorus Strait to Üsküdar in Asia.

The tram route of most interest to visitors is the T1 between Bağcılar and Kabataş, which links the Old City and Sultanahmet with the shopping, gallery and nightlife districts across the Golden Horn in Galata and Beyoğlu. The T1 tram links in with the metro system at Karaköy (for the Tünel funicular) and Kabataş (for the funicular to Taksim Square and ferry terminal for the Princes' Islands). A period tram runs up and down Istiklal Caddesi between Tünel and Taksim Square.

Travelling by Funicular

The Tünel, connecting Karaköy to İstiklal Caddesi (see p86), the city's main shopping and entertainment street, is one of the world's oldest undergrounds. Another funicular runs from the Bosphorus shore at Kabataş to Taksim Square.

Travelling by Bus

Municipal buses are often crowded, the drivers usually only speak Turkish and the schedules are unreliable. Sometimes, however, they are the only public transport available – running up the European or Asian shores of the Bosphorus, for example – so some visitors may want to make the effort to use them.

Travelling by Ferry

It is a pleasure to travel around Istanbul's waterways by ferry. The main dock at Eminönü has departures to the Asian suburbs of Üsküdar and Kadıköy, and up the Golden Horn. It is also the departure point for Bosphorus cruise excursions (see pp34–5). Ferries for Asia also depart from Karaköy. Ferries to the Princes' Islands run from Eminönü, Beşiktaş and Kadıköy but are scheduled to depart from the new Kabataş terminal, at the northern end of the T1 tram line, from 2020. Ferries are run by **City Lines** (Şehir Hatları). Sea buses, operated by **Istanbul Sea Buses** (IDO), run from Istanbul Yenikapı across the Sea of Marmara and to the Princes' Islands.

Tickets

Buy tokens for buses, the metro, tram and ferries from kiosks near stations and stops. Alternatively the Istanbulkart travel smart card can be used on all of these and saves around 25 per cent per journey. As you enter the form of transport, touch the reader with your card and recharge the card when necessary. The card deposit fee is nominal and you can load credit from kiosks, stations or vending machines.

Travelling by Taxi

A licensed taxi (taksi) is yellow in colour and shows a light on top when it is available for hire. Before you set off, always check that the meter is switched on. Better still, agree the fare with your driver before you get in. Day and night rides are charged at the same rate. Beware of drivers taking the long way around in order to short-change you or those who wish to drop you off at the wrong location to avoid traffic. Some will not take short trips as the journey time is often increased due to congestion.

Travelling by Dolmuş

These shared minibuses run along set routes, and only depart when they are full. They will stop wherever you want along the route. Ranks have a blue sign with a black D on a white background. Several useful dolmuş services leave from around Taksim Square. They are a cheap form of transport, but can make for a slow journey.

Travelling by Car

Driving in the city centre is a nightmare. The larger business hotels have parking, but most in the Old City do not. Hire a car and driver to see sights that are further apart.

Travelling on Foot

Walking is a great way to see the city, especially the historic core bounded by the Theodosian Walls. Unfortunately streets are often unmarked, so it's easy to wander off track. Pavements may be rough and uneven, and kerbs high, so wear good shoes or boots. Traffic only stops at controlled crossings.

DIRECTORY

ARRIVING BY AIR
Havabüs
(0212) 444 26 56
w havabus.com

HAVAIST
(0212) 219 53 52
w hava.ist

Istanbul Airport
Arnavütköy
(0212) 444 14 42
w istanbulhavalimani.com

Sabiha Gökçen
Pendik
(0216) 588 88 88
w sabihagokcen.aero

ARRIVING BY COACH
Esenler
(0212) 658 05 05

Eurolines
UK: 08717 818181
w eurolines.com

Harem
(0216) 333 37 63

ARRIVING BY RAIL
Man in Seat 61
w maninseat61.com

TRAVELLING BY METRO AND TRAM
Istanbulkart
w istanbulkart.iett.gov.tr

Metro İstanbul
(0212) 568 99 70
w metro.istanbul

TRAVELLING BY BUS
Municipal buses
(0212) 372 22 22
w iett.gov.tr

TRAVELLING BY FERRY
City Lines
(0212) 444 18 51
w sehirhatlari.com.tr

Istanbul Sea Buses
0850 222 4436
w ido.com.tr

Practical Information

Passports and Visas

To enter Turkey, you need a full passport valid for at least six months. Most people requiring a visa must apply in advance online through the **e-Visa** portal. The cost depends on your nationality: **UK** ($20), **US** ($20), Canada ($60), **Australia** ($60) and Ireland ($20). Payment can be made by debit or credit card.

A multiple-entry tourist visa valid for up to 90 days in 180 days will be issued. South Africans or people with British National Overseas passports must apply for a visa at a consulate before travelling. New Zealand nationals receive a free tourist visa on arrival that is valid for up to three months. Requirements can change so check with the **Turkish Ministry of Foreign Affairs** for the latest information.

Customs and Immigration

Visitors may bring up to 50 cigars, 600 cigarettes, 200 g (7 oz) tobacco, 1 litre spirits, 2 litres wine, 2 kg (4 lbs) chocolate, tea and coffee, 600 ml perfume and unlimited currency. Penalties for possessing narcotics are very harsh.

Travel Safety Advice

Visitors can get up-to-date safety information from the **UK Foreign and Commonwealth Office**, the **US Department of State** and the **Australian Department of Foreign Affairs and Trade**.

Travel Insurance

You are strongly advised to take out travel insurance with full medical cover, including repatriation by air. If buying a Europe-only policy, check that it will also cover you on the Asian side of Istanbul.

Health

Before going to Istanbul, make sure your basic inoculations are up-to-date, and check with your doctor about Hepatitis A and Hepatitis B vaccinations.

Rabies is prevalent in Turkey, so be wary of the city's many stray dogs and cats. Mosquitoes can be a problem in summer, so take some repellent. While Istanbul tap water is considered safe, it is advisable to drink bottled water. If you have a sensitive stomach, you should avoid salads and seafood from street stalls.

There are numerous pharmacies *(eczane)* across the city. Duty *(nobetçi)* chemists, often stationed near hospitals, are open all night. The state hospital system is fine in an emergency, but private hospitals are more efficient. Well-regarded hospitals include the **Amerikan Hastanesi** (American Hospital), the **Alman Hastanesi** (German Hospital), **Cerrahpaşa Hastanesi** and **Sen Jorj Avustrya Hastanesi** (St George's Austrian Hospital).

Turkish dentists are well-trained and many have the latest equipment. Fees are relatively low and some visitors come to Istanbul just to have their teeth fixed. **Prodent-Can Ergene** and **Reha Sezgin** are recommended clinics.

Personal Security

Istanbul has a low crime rate, but take precautions against pickpockets, particularly on the crowded public transport system and busy shopping areas. Districts with bad reputations include Tarlabaşı, near Taksim Square, where prostitution and petty theft are a problem, and the Theodosian Walls *(see p42)*, where vagrants and alcoholics are a nuisance towards dusk. Lone men should beware of confidence tricksters in nightclubs, especially around Taksim Square, who trick the unwary into buying expensive drinks for attractive women. The spiking of drinks is not unknown, either.

Terrorism is a potential threat, with a number of terrorist attacks in the city in 2016. The last attack was in January 2017, at a Boshphorus-front nightclub. Visitors should avoid protests, which often take place along İstiklal Caddesi and up to Taksim Square (the scene of the Gezi Park protests) as violent confrontations between riot police and demonstrators are not uncommon.

Do not joke, make light of or criticize Turkey, its founding father, Atatürk, or the country's flag, as the majority of Turks are very nationalistic and will take offence. Defacing a banknote (invariably adorned with an image of Atatürk) or the flag is a criminal offence.

Turkey has become more conservative in recent years, with women in headscarves a common sight, and stricter restrictions for non-Muslims when visiting mosques. Couples should beware of displaying affection in public, and never make jokes about Islam.

Many younger women, particularly Istanbulites, dress much as they would anywhere else in Europe. Foreign women out for the night in areas like Beyoğlu often do likewise. However, such dress is not appropriate in many parts of the city, or when visiting mosques. Women who are travelling alone should be extra-careful; dress conservatively, don't make eye contact with men and avoid backstreets, especially at night. If you are being harassed, make a scene and someone will come to your aid. The Turkish police are usually polite and helpful.

Homosexuality is not illegal in Turkey, but it is frowned upon by Islam. There is a thriving LGBT+ scene in Istanbul, but there is significant homophobia. A pride march takes place near Taksim Square every year, either in June or in July. Visitors can check out **Gays of Turkey** and **Lambda** for more details.

Emergency Services

In tourist areas, report losses, theft or other problems to the **Tourist Police** – translators are usually present from 9am to 5pm Monday to Friday. It is illegal to be out in public without photo ID; keep a of copy your passport with you. If you get into trouble, most countries have consulates in Istanbul – they will help with missing documents, arrange repatriation, or help you find legal representation if needed.

Istanbul is in a major earthquake zone, and the last serious quake to take place was in 1999. As a result, building rules and regulations were tightened up and existing buildings have been retro-quake-proofed. But still today many of the city's structures – especially older ones – are not adequately quakeproofed.

In the event of an emergency, contact the **police**, the **fire** department or call an **ambulance** (also for general emergencies).

DIRECTORY

PASSPORTS AND VISAS

Australia
Asker Ocağı Cad 15, Elmadağ, Şişli
((0212) 243 13 33

e-Visa
w evisa.gov.tr

Turkish Ministry of Foreign Affairs
w mfa.gov.tr

UK
MAP J5 ■ Meşrutiyet Cad 34, Tepebaşı, Beyoğlu
((0212) 334 64 00

US
İstinye Mahallesi, Kaplıcalar Mevkii No. 2, İstinye
((0212) 335 90 00

TRAVEL SAFETY ADVICE

Australian Department of Foreign Affairs and Trade
w dfat.gov.au
w smarttraveller.gov.au

UK Foreign and Commonwealth Office
w gov.uk/foreign-travel-advice

US Department of State
w travel.state.gov

HEALTH

Alman Hastanesi
MAP L5 ■ Sıraselviler Cad 119, Taksim
((0212) 293 21 50

Amerikan Hastanesi
Güzelbahçe Sok 20, Nişantaşı
w amerikanhastanesi.com.tr

Cerrahpaşa Hastanesi
Koca Mustafapaşa Cad, Cerrahpaşa
w cerrahpasa.istanbulc.edu.tr

Prodent-Can Ergene
Valikonağı Cad 109/5, Nişantaşı
w prodent.com.tr

Reha Sezgin
Halaskargazi Cad 48/9, Harbiye
((0212) 240 33 22

Sen Jorj Avustrya Hastanesi
MAP F3 ■ Bereketzade Medresesi Sok 7, Galata
w sjh.com.tr

PERSONAL SECURITY

Gays of Turkey
w gaysofturkey.com

Lambda
w lambdaistanbul

EMERGENCY SERVICES

Ambulance
(112

Fire
(110

Police
(155

Tourist Police
MAP R4 ■ Yerebatan Cad 6, Sultanahmet
w iem.gov.tr

Travellers with Specific Needs

The city is quite difficult to navigate in a wheelchair owing to steep hills, high kerbs and cobbled roads. However, things have improved in recent years. The tram and metro lines are wheelchair accessible. Many of the major sites such as the Haghia Sophia and Blue Mosque are partially accessible, and many hotels have one or more specially-adapted rooms and wheelchair access to most floors. The **Turkish Culture and Tourism Office (UK)** has a helpful website for travellers with specific requirements.

Currency and Banking

The Turkish lira (TL) comes in 5, 10, 20, 50, 100 and 200 lira notes and 1 lira coins. One lira is split into 100 *kuruş*, which come in 1, 5, 10, 25 and 50 *kuruş* coins. You are allowed to bring unlimited foreign currency and up to US\$5,000 worth of lira into Turkey, but you'll get a better exchange rate in Turkey. Note that the ₺ sign, introduced in 2012, is widely used, but many places still use the old TL (Türk Lirası) short-hand, e.g 5 TL.

Make sure that you have plenty of small-denomination notes and coins with you at all times to make small purchases. Most souvenir shops are happy to accept lira, US dollars, euros or pounds sterling. Your change will come in lira.

There are plenty of banks in the city but changing money can be slow. The many 24-hour cash dispensers (ATMs) accept all Maestro and Cirrus bank cards with a PIN, and will also give a cash advance on credit cards. Most ATMs are programmed with several languages; some pay out in a range of currencies.

If you have cash to exchange, the best place to go is an exchange office (*döviz*). These kiosks are found in all the main tourist areas. They are faster and usually offer a better rate of exchange than the banks. Most outlets dealing with tourists will accept major credit cards such as Visa and MasterCard.

Telephone and Internet

Turkey's mobile phone system is compatible with UK phones, but US cell phones may not work. To save on charges, buy a local pay-as-you-go SIM or an international card from agencies such as **TravelSim**. The few remaining public phones accept credit cards or a phone card bought from a post office. Hotel phones are usually expensive.

The international dialling code for Turkey is +90. Istanbul has two area codes: 0212 for the European side and 0216 for the Asian side. To call abroad from Istanbul, dial 00 followed by the country code (61 for Australia, 1 for the United States and 44 for the UK).

Virtually all of Istanbul's hotels have free Wi-Fi, though some international chains do charge for the service. Many of the city's cafés have free Wi-Fi.

Postal Services

Post offices and boxes can be recognized by a yellow and blue PTT (Post Telegraf Telefon) logo. Stamps can only be bought at post offices and **PTT** kiosks. The most useful post offices for visitors are the **Old City Post Office** and the **Beyoğlu Post Office**, both open 8:30am–7pm daily. The post can be slow, so if you wish to send purchases home, use a courier. All the main courier firms have offices in Istanbul and there are also some reliable domestic ones such as **Aras** and Yurtiçi.

TV, Radio and Newspapers

TVs are standard in the majority of Istanbul hotels. Most show BBC World, CNN and other international news channels, and many also show entertainment channels such as BBC Entertainment, National Geographic and the Discovery Channel.

There are two English-language Turkish daily newspapers, the *Hürriyet Daily News* and *Daily Sabah*. Magazine-wise, *The Guide Istanbul* (bimonthly) and *Time Out* (monthly) have entertainment and dining listings. *Cornucopia* covers the arts, history and general culture of Turkey.

Opening Hours

Banks in main tourist areas open 8:30am–5pm Monday to Friday; a few larger branches also open on Saturday mornings and all have 24-hour cash dispensers. Post offices open 9am–5pm Monday to Saturday. Shops are open 10am–6pm Monday to Saturday, with many tourist shops and larger shops staying open for longer. Malls open 10am–10pm.

Museum and sight opening times vary quite a bit, though 9am–5pm is a useful guideline. The majority of the more important museums and major attractions such as Haghia Sophia and Topkapı Place are open by an hour or two longer between April and October than they are between November and March.

There are five official one-day state holidays (see p57); 1 January is New Year's Day, 23 April is National Sovereignty and Children's Day, 19 May is Youth & Sports Day, 30 August is Victory Day and 29 October is Republic Day.

Istanbulites celebrate two principal religious festivals: Şeker Bayramı, which follows the holy month of Ramazan (Ramadan), and Kurban Bayramı (see p57). During Ramazan, no water or food is allowed during daylight hours. Nothing actually shuts down, but daily life is disrupted. The dates of Ramazan, Şeker Bayramı and Kurban Bayramı move backwards by 11 days each year.

Time Difference

Turkey is 3 hours ahead of Greenwich Mean Time, 7 hours ahead of the US East Coast, 10 hours ahead of the US West Coast and 7 hours behind Australia.

Electrical Appliances

The current is 220V, and plugs have two round pins. You'll need a transformer to use 110V appliances from the US.

Weather

Summers are sunny and dry, with the odd thunderstorm. It can reach 40° C (104° F), but 31–33° C (88–91° F) is normal at noon in August, dropping to around 23° C (74° F) at night. Winter can be cool and damp, with some snow and January temperatures of around 8° C (46° F) at midday and 2° C (36° F) overnight. In April, May, June and September/October, the weather is ideal for exploring on foot.

Visitor Information

There are several official tourist offices and kiosks around the city. The most convenient **tourist office** for a majority of visitors is in Sultanahmet, near the Hippodrome, which is open 9am–5pm daily. The staff here speak English and can provide you with useful city maps for free.

For general tourist information about the city, the **Turkish Ministry of Tourism and Culture** has useful websites, and **Turkey Travel Planner** is a good independent website. For those looking to book tickets to shows and events, **Biletix** is indispensable.

DIRECTORY

TRAVELLERS WITH SPECIFIC NEEDS
Turkish Culture and Tourism Office (UK)
w gototurkey.co.uk

TELEPHONE AND INTERNET
TravelSim
w travelsim.co.uk

POSTAL SERVICES
Aras
📞 444 2552
w araskargo.com.tr
Beyoğlu Post Office
MAP K5 « Yeni Çarşı Cad, Beyoğlu
📞 (0212) 251 51 50
Old City Post Office
MAP Q2 « Büyük Postane Cad, Sirkeci
📞 (0212) 526 12 00
PTT
w ptt.gov.tr
Yurtiçi
📞 444 9999
w yurticikargo.com

TV, RADIO AND NEWSPAPERS
Cornucopia
w cornucopia.net
Daily Sabah
w dailysabah.com
The Guide Istanbul
w theguideistanbul.com
Hürriyet Daily News
w hurriyetdailynews.com
Time Out
w timeoutistanbul.com

VISITOR INFORMATION
Biletix
w biletix.com
Tourist Office
MAP Q4 ■ Divanyolu 3, Sultanahmet
📞 (0212) 518 87 54
Turkey Travel Planner
w turkeytravelplanner.com
Turkish Ministry of Tourism and Culture
w gototurkey.co.uk
w kultur.gov.tr

Language and Religion

In tourist areas, there will always be someone who speaks some English. Written Turkish uses the Western alphabet, but there are some differences in pronunciation. C is pronounced "*j*" as in "jam", ç is "*ch*" as in "church" and ş is "*sh*" as in "shut". İ is used as in "igloo"; the dotless "i" (ı) is more like "*uh*". The ğ is silent, but is used to draw out the preceding vowel. Ninety-nine per cent of Turks are Muslim, but the degree to which they practise their religion varies.

Toilets

There are still relatively few modern public conveniences (*bay* for men, *bayan* for women) in the city. Some have squat toilets only. Carry tissues, as there may not always be paper. Most mosques have squat toilets attached. There is usually a charge of around ₺2 to use these facilities. Most sights, cafés and restaurants have Western-style toilets.

Trips and Tours

Most travel agents and tour operators in Turkey will be happy to provide a private guide in one of half a dozen major languages. The guide should be accredited by the Ministry of Tourism. Some licensed guides (check the ID around their necks) tout for business outside major sights. It is advisable to visit the **Istanbul Chamber of Tour Guides** website before hiring a guide.

Many agencies offer tours by bus, boat, on foot or a mix of all three, with full- and half-day options. Trips to sights such as Gallipoli and Troy, Edirne or Bursa are also available. Reliable tour companies include **Cooking Alaturka**, **Turkish Flavours**, **Fest Travel**, **Istanbul Walks** and **Istanbul Tour Studio**. **Big Bus City Tours** do open-topped double-decker hop-on, hop-off tours of the city.

Shopping

Traditionally, Istanbulites shop in bazaars. Most famous is the historic Grand Bazaar (*see pp22–3*), a covered "mall" of over 4,000 shops dating back several hundred years. It is full of everything from fine quality Turkish carpets and jewellery to fake designer goods and touristy souvenirs. The Spice Bazaar (*see p52*) is equally venerable and is excellent for spices, dried fruit and nuts and much more. The Arasta Bazaar (*see p52*) is good for authentic souvenirs such as İznik pottery and *peştemal* (*hamam* towels). Haggling in places like this is part of daily life. Take your time, shop around and don't feel pressurized. When you are ready, offer half the price and take it from there.

For European-style clothes shopping, head across the Golden Horn to İstiklal Caddesi, or to the posh suburbs of Nişantaşı and Teşvikiye. The best and/or most convenient of the city's 90 malls are **Kanyon** (*see p53*), the Zorlu Centre (*see p53*), **City's Mall** or **Demirören**. Don't bargain for goods in upmarket shops or shopping malls.

VAT (KDV in Turkish) is included in fixed-price goods. There are various rates, but the most common is 18 per cent. Prices may rise if you ask for a VAT invoice – a trader who writes an invoice will have to pay tax. To reclaim tax on departure, shop at places displaying a tax-free sign and get a Global Refund Cheque to reclaim the tax (in cash) at the airport. You may be asked to produce the goods, so keep them with you.

Dining

The very finest of Turkey's renowned cuisine can be found in the metropolis of Istanbul. Places to eat in Sultanahmet are not always the greatest – try to head further afield for a more authentic Istanbul culinary experience. Children are welcomed in all but the smartest places, but don't expect to find highchairs.

Lokantas are day-to-day eateries. They range from self-service cafeterias to full-service brasserie-style places, invariably serving stew-type dishes from steam trays, though they often have grills as well. Prices are affordable; few serve alcohol. A *restoran* is upmarket; if you see the word *balık*, the place specializes in fish and seafood. A *kebapçı* serves kebabs and *lahmacun*, a thin, round flatbread with a savoury mince topping; a *dönerci*, döner kebabs and other roast meats. A *pideci* is the Turkish equivalent of a pizzeria, though the Turkish *pide* does not have a tomato sauce layer; it is usually cheese or meat only.

For a drink and live music with a meal, usually an array of *meze* (Turkish tapas) followed by grilled fish, try a *meyhane*. To try a hookah pipe, head for a *nargile* café, where you'll be plied with sweet tea while you suck on a water-pipe. Simple *kahvehanes* (tearooms) are generally a male preserve, where men spend their time playing games of back-gammon. Some cafés have a separate section for women and families (*aile salonu*) at the back, as do some restaurants.

Turks often eat desserts separately to main meals; a *muhallebici* sells milk puddings; *pastanes* sell pastries, such as baklava. Look out for patisseries where you can sit down and sample baklava or cake with a shot of Turkish coffee.

Bars in Sultanahmet are very touristy; head across the Golden Horn to Galata and Beyoğlu for lively drinking joints ranging from studenty dives to chic rooftop bars.

Few restaurants in Istanbul cater specifically to vegetarians, though there are few places in Beyoğlu. Good options for vegetarians are *pide*, Turkish pizzas dripping with a Cheddar-cheese-type topping, or goat's cheese with parsley. The stews and soups served at *lokantas* are often virtually vegetarian, but usually have a meat stock. There are dozens of veggie *meze* in decent *meyhanes*.

If a service charge (*servis dahil*) isn't added to your bill, leave a 10 per cent tip.

Accommodation

On the whole, the standard of accommodation is high, and most places are good value. Sultanahmet and some areas adjoining it are Istanbul tourist heartland, and there are several hundred hotels here. Options range from cheap-and-cheerful hostels to luxury hotels, boutique hotels fashioned from period Ottoman town houses and not especially characterful hotels that are comfortable and well run. Across the Golden Horn in Galata and Beyoğlu are many more choices, ranging from hip hostels to late 19th-century European-style hotels such as the famed Pera Palace (*see p83*). There are lots of apartments for rent here too. This district is usually favoured by those as interested in shopping, dining and gallery-hopping as they are by historic sights. Period luxury hotels fronting the Bosphorus are very popular and expensive.

It pays to book early, as many hotels now work on a yield-management system. A lot of hotels also offer decent discounts for bookings, which are made through their own website (though this doesn't mean you can't find a better buy on one of the standard online booking sites, such as **Expedia**) and for bookings paid by cash. Room prices tend to drop dramatically out of season (November to early March, excluding Christmas and New Year).

Places to Stay

PRICE CATEGORIES
For a standard, double room per night (with breakfast if included), taxes and extra charges.
....
₺ under ₺400   ₺₺ ₺400–1000   ₺₺₺ over ₺1000

Luxury Hotels

Ceylan InterContinental, Taksim

MAP B5 ▪ Asker Ocağı Cad 1 ▪ (0212) 368 44 44 ▪ www.intercontinental.com.tr ▪ ₺₺
This hilltop tower offers some of the finest views in the city. It has 382 rooms and suites, plus a bar, restaurants, a health club and a 24-hour business centre. Join Istanbul high society for tea with live music in the botanic garden or tea lounge.

Conrad Istanbul, Beşiktaş

MAP C5 ▪ Saray Cad 5 ▪ (0212) 310 25 25 ▪ www.conradistanbul.com ▪ ₺₺
Each of the 590 rooms in this huge hotel has a view. The facilities are second to none, and the furnishings chic. Its bars and restaurants offer Italian and Turkish cuisine.

Eresin Hotel, Sultanahmet

MAP Q6 ▪ Küçük Ayasofya Cad 40 ▪ (0212) 638 44 28 ▪ www.eresin.com.tr ▪ ₺₺
Standing on the site of the great Byzantine Palace, this luxurious hotel has its own museum. All 60 rooms and suites have parquet floors and Jacuzzi baths. There are two restaurants, a bar and a terrace that offers lovely sea views.

The Marmara Pera, Tepebaşı

MAP J5 ▪ Meşrutiyet Cad 1 ▪ (0212) 334 03 00 ▪ www.themarmarahotels.com ▪ ₺₺
Situated in the heart of Beyoğlu, with a signature café-restaurant and rooftop pool, this chic hotel has fabulous floor-to-ceiling windows in every room.

Four Seasons Hotel, Sultanahmet

MAP R5 ▪ Tevkifhane Sok 1 ▪ (0212) 402 30 00 ▪ www.fourseasons.com ▪ ₺₺₺
The sheer opulence of the Four Seasons belies its past as an Ottoman prison. The 65 rooms are furnished with antiques and kilims, there is a health club, a magnificent glass-roofed restaurant and superb views over the Sea of Marmara.

Hyatt Regency, Taksim

MAP B5 ▪ Taşkışla Cad ▪ (0212) 368 12 34 ▪ www.hyatt.com ▪ ₺₺₺
All 360 rooms and suites at this elegantly decorated resort offer great views. There is also a health club, pool, tennis courts and business facilities.

Park Hyatt, Teşvikiye

MAP B4 ▪ Bronz Sok 4, Teşvikiye ▪ (0212) 315 12 34 ▪ www.hyatt.com ▪ ₺₺₺
Located in a busy shopping district, this stylish boutique hotel has 90 spacious rooms and suites. There is also a spa and a fitness centre.

Raffles Istanbul

MAP C4 ▪ Zorlu Centre, Zincirlikuyu ▪ (0212) 924 02 00 ▪ www.raffles.com/Istanbul ▪ ₺₺₺
Part of a contemporary shopping and performing arts centre, Raffles is luxury incarnate. Many rooms have a panoramic view of the Bosphorus. Personal butlers attend to guests' needs and there is also a spa in the hotel. Among the number of restaurants and bars on the premises is a Michelin-star Spanish restaurant.

Ritz-Carlton, Şişli

MAP B5 ▪ Süzer Plaza, Elmadağ ▪ (0212) 334 44 44 ▪ www.ritzcarlton.com ▪ ₺₺₺
"Ritz" is considered a byword for luxury, and the Istanbul hotel's 244 rooms and suites more than live up to expectation. There's a whisky and cigar bar too.

Large Upmarket Hotels

Germir Palas

MAP Y2 ▪ Cumhuriyet Cad 7, Taksim ▪ (0212) 361 11 10 ▪ www.germirpalas.com ▪ ₺
The entrance to this gem on Beyoğlu's main street is easy to miss. The lobby and bars are plush, and the rooms are well decorated with interesting textiles. The terrace restaurant is great to dine at in the summer and boasts fine views over the Bosphorus.

Best Western Eresin Taxim Hotel, Taksim

MAP B5 ▪ Topçu Cad 16 ▪ (0212) 256 08 03 ▪ www.eresintaxim.com.tr ▪ ₺₺
This four-star hotel has 70 rooms and suites, some of which include triples. Guests can also ask for hypoallergenic and orthopaedic pillows. The lounge bar has live piano music in the evenings.

The Marmara Istanbul, Taksim

MAP L4 ▪ Taksim Meydanı ▪ (0212) 334 83 00 ▪ www.themarmarahotels.com ▪ ₺₺
A large, modern hotel situated on Taksim Square, The Marmara offers 376 comfortable rooms with city views, as well as a fully equipped gym, outdoor pool, *hamam* and several top-class restaurants.

Mövenpick Hotel Istanbul, Levent

MAP U2 ▪ Büyükdere Cad 4, Levent ▪ (0212) 319 29 29 ▪ www.movenpickhotel.com ▪ ₺₺
This five-star hilltop hotel with 249 rooms and suites offers great views and smooth service. GourmeT, the hotel's café in the lobby, serves sumptuous chocolates, cakes and Mövenpick ice cream.

Radisson Blu Bosphorus Hotel, Ortaköy

MAP C4 ▪ Çırağan Cad 46 ▪ (0212) 310 15 00 ▪ www.radissonblu.com ▪ ₺₺
The location is the real winner here – the peaceful village of Ortaköy, beside the Bosphorus. This hotel has a patio restaurant overlooking the water, and 120 rooms with contemporary decor. Allow plenty of time when taking taxis into town during rush hour.

Renaissance Polat Istanbul Hotel, Yeşilyurt

Sahilyolu Cad 2 ▪ (0212) 414 18 00 ▪ www.marriott.com ▪ ₺₺
Located close to the and World Trade Centre, this 416-room hotel has a luxury pool and health club. There are also fine restaurants, bars and cafés, and good business facilities.

Swissôtel The Bosphorus, Maçka

MAP B5 ▪ Bayıldım Cad 2 ▪ (0212) 326 11 00 ▪ www.swissotel.com ▪ ₺₺
On a hilltop with views of the Bosphorus, this hotel has 585 rooms and suites, a wellness centre, shopping arcade, restaurants and rooftop bars.

Taxim Suites, Taksim

MAP B5 ▪ Cumhuriyet Cad 31 ▪ (0212) 254 77 77 ▪ www.taximsuites.com ▪ ₺₺
These 20 fully serviced suites are good for those who need a bit more space, giving you a one-bed apartment for less than the cost of a five-star hotel room. With Taksim Square on the doorstep, there are plenty of places to eat nearby.

Hyatt Regency Istanbul Ataköy

Sahilyolu ▪ (0212) 463 12 34 ▪ www.hyatt.com ▪ ₺₺₺
This hotel is situated on the shores of the Sea of Marmara in the Bakırköy district. Facilities include tennis courts, swimming pool and meeting rooms. There is a shuttle bus to Sultanahmet.

Hilton Hotel, Harbiye

MAP B5 ▪ Cumhuriyet Cad ▪ (0212) 315 60 00 ▪ www.hilton.com ▪ ₺₺₺
Conveniently located for Taksim and the business districts, this grand hotel has 498 rooms, fitness centre, tennis courts, two pools, hamam, conference facilities and much more.

Characterful Hotels – Sultanahmet and the Old City

Hotel Kybele

MAP R4 ▪ Yerebatan Cad 35 ▪ (0212) 511 77 66/7 ▪ www.kybelehotel.com ▪ ₺
Intimate, family-run and friendly, and a couple of steps from Divanyolu, this Aladdin's cave of a hotel is a treasure trove of Turkish history, with hundreds of lamps and other Ottoman antiques decorating the public rooms, 16 bedrooms and garden.

Hotel Sarı Konak

MAP R5 ▪ Mimar Mehmet Ağa Cad 26 ▪ (0212) 638 62 58 ▪ www.istanbulhotelsarikonak.com ▪ ₺
The owners of this 19-room hotel pride themselves on providing their guests a "home away from home". The café offers 360° views, and breakfast is served in a beautiful Byzantine courtyard.

Kariye Hotel, Edirnekapı

MAP J2 ▪ Kariye Camii
Sok 6 ▪ (0212) 534 84 14
▪ www.kariyeotel.com ▪ ₺
This late 19th-century
wooden mansion has 27
rooms and suites (with
modern amenities), a
garden overlooking
the Golden Horn and
renowned restaurant
Asitane (see p79).

Blue House Hotel

MAP R5 ▪ Dalbastı Sok
14 ▪ (0212) 638 90 10
▪ www.blue-house-hotel.
hotel-istanbul.net ▪ ₺₺
In a quiet street behind
the Arasta Bazaar, this
hotel has 26 rooms, all
with superb views.

Hotel Dersaadet

MAP Q6 ▪ Küçük
Ayasofya Cad, Kapıağası
Sok 5 ▪ (0212) 458 07
60/1 ▪ www.dersaadet
hotel.com ▪ ₺₺
Set at the foot of the
hill behind Sultanahmet
Square, this Ottoman
house offers superb views
of the Old City or the sea
from all 17 rooms.

Hotel Empress Zöe

MAP R5 ▪ Akbıyık Cad
10, Sultanahmet ▪ (0212)
518 43 60/25 04 ▪ www.
emzoe.com ▪ ₺₺
Old houses surround a
lush garden and ruins of
a 15th-century bathhouse
at this delightful hotel. Its
25 rooms and suites are
decorated in Turkish style.

Ibrahim Pasha

MAP Q5 ▪ Terzihane Sok,
5 Adliye Yanı ▪ (0212) 518
03 95 ▪ www.ibrahim
pasha.com ▪ ₺₺
A couple of 19th-century
townhouses, on a side
street running off the
historic Hippodrome,
have been converted
into a superb, ultra-
friendly boutique hotel.
Room decor combines
Ottoman opulence with
contemporary elegance.
There is a lounge area
with an open fire and
a library downstairs.

Neorion Orhaniye

MAP F4 ▪ Cad 14, Sirkeci
▪ (0212) 527 90 90 ▪ www.
neorionhotel.com ▪ ₺₺
Neo-Ottoman in style, this
hotel is located between
Sultanahmet (see p60)
and the Golden Horn (see
p74) waterfront. A base-
ment pool and a spa are
also present, alongside
some comfy rooms.

Niles Hotel

MAP E5 ▪ Dibekli Cami
Sok 13 ▪ (0212) 517 32
39 ▪ www.hotelniles.
com ▪ ₺₺
Located near the
main tourist areas of
Sultanahmet, this hotel
offers great value with
compact yet tasteful
rooms, an excellent roof-
top restaurant with sea
views and friendly staff.

Sarnıç Hotel

MAP Q6 ▪ Küçük Ayasofya
Cad 26 ▪ (0212) 518 23
23 ▪ www.sarnichotel.
com ▪ ₺₺
This 21-room hotel behind
the Blue Mosque (see
pp18–19) has a rooftop
terrace restaurant. Guests
can see the 5th-century
Byzantine cistern (sarnıç)
under the hotel.

Turkoman

MAP Q5 ▪ Asmalı Çeşme
Sok 2 ▪ (0212) 516 29
56 ▪ www.turkoman
hotel.com ▪ ₺₺
A lovely boutique hotel,
Turkoman is set in a
period building close
to the Hippodrome (see
p42). The rooms have
wooden flooring, brass
beds and Turkish rugs,
and there's a roof terrace
with stunning views.

Best Western Acropol Hotel

MAP R5 ▪ Akbıyık Cad 21
▪ (0212) 638 90 21 ▪ www.
acropol.com ▪ ₺₺₺
The 28 rooms in this
restored Ottoman house
have wooden floors and
painted ceilings – but also
Wi-Fi and double glazing.
The fifth-floor restaurant
has fine views. Other
facilities at the hotel
include a café, TV room,
fitness club and Turkish
hamam. Free airport
transfers are also avail-
able for guests.

Characterful Hotels – Galata, Beyoğlu and Around

Hotel Villa Zurich, Cihangir

MAP G2 ▪ Akarsu Yokuşu
Cad 36 ▪ (0212) 293 06 04
▪ www.hotelvillazurich.
com ▪ ₺
Just a short walk from
Taksim Square, this
42-room hotel has a
breakfast terrace with
views of the Bosphorus.

10 Karaköy

Kemeraltı Cad 10,
Karaköy ▪ (0212) 703
33 33 ▪ www.morgans
hotelgroup.com ▪ ₺₺
Located close to the
Galata Bridge, the Morgan
Group's first venture (see
p70) in Istanbul is fash-
ioned from a 19th-century
Neo-Classical building
that combines sleek
decor with period style.
Guests can relax in the
elegant bar on the roof.

Anemon Galata, Beyoğlu

MAP F2 ■ Büyük Hendek Cad 5, Kuledibi ■ (0212) 293 23 43 ■ www.anemon hotels.com ■ ₺₺
Set in a restored Art Nouveau mansion, this 27-room hotel is just a short walk from Beyoğlu's shopping and nightlife.

Bankerhan Hotel

MAP F3 ■ Banker Sok 2, Beyoğlu ■ (0212) 243 56 17 ■ www.bankerhan. com ■ ₺₺
Full of contemporary art works, this designer hotel is set in an atmospheric 19th-century townhouse. It is located close to Beyoğlu's nightclubs (see p88) and is a short walk from the Galata Bridge (see p70).

Pera Palace Hotel

MAP J5 ■ Meşrutiyet Cad 52, Beyoğlu ■ (0212) 377 40 00 ■ www.pera palace.com ■ ₺₺
This 19th-century hotel (see p83) once catered to prestigious passengers who arrived on the Orient Express, including Agatha Christie and Graham Green. It retains its old-world charm but has all the modern amenities needed for a great stay.

SuB

Necatibey Cad 21, Karaköy ■ (0212) 243 00 05 ■ www.sub karakoy.com ■ ₺₺
The rooms here have been individually designed, with a mix of industrial grunge and homely touches, such as wraparound headboards and natural pine floors. Excellent terrace bar and café complete the picture.

Tom Tom Suites

MAP K6 ■ Tomtom Kaptan Sk 18 ■ (0212) 292 49 49 ■ www.tom tomsuites.com ■ ₺₺
Occupying a former Franciscan nunnery, Tom Tom Suites provide some of the most stylish rooms in Beyoğlu. Located opposite the Italian consulate on a quiet street, the rooms have en-suite bathrooms with marble-clad walls, high-ceilings and muted contemporary furnishings. Some upper-floor rooms have lovely Bosphorus views.

Triada Residence

MAP L4 ■ Meşelik Sok 4, İstiklal Cad ■ (0212) 251 01 01 ■ www.triada-residence.inistanbul hotels.com ■ ₺₺
Triada is well-located opposite the monumental Greek Orthodox Church of Haghia Triada. The cosy but contemporary rooms have pale walls adorned with tasteful prints and photographs, contrasting with heavily grained wooden floors and furniture. There are large flat-screen TVs in all rooms.

Vault Karaköy

MAP F3 ■ Bankalar Cad 5, Karaköy ■ (0212) 244 34 00 ■ www.thehousehotel. com ■ ₺₺
A grandiose 19th-century bank in hip Karaköy has been converted into this boutique hotel run by the well-regarded House group. Many of the original features have been retained, including granite floors and tall, elegant windows. The vault itself is now stocked with fine wines.

Georges Hotel

MAP J6 ■ Serdar-ı Ekrem Cad 24, Beyoğlu ■ (0212) 244 24 23 ■ www. georges.com ■ ₺₺₺
A small hotel with a roof terrace, Georges is set in a historic building. The rooms are all individually styled, and some have attached balconies with views of the sea.

Budget Hotels and Self-Catering

Büyük (Grand) Londra, Beyoğlu

MAP J5 ■ Meşrutiyet Cad 53 ■ (0212) 245 06 70 ■ www.londrahotel.net ■ ₺
Faded decadence at its most alluring, the Londra has been around since the 1900s. Ernest Hemingway stayed here and the Turkish hit film *Head On* featured the hotel. Some of the eccentrically decorated rooms overlook the Golden Horn.

Cheers Lighthouse

MAP F6 ■ Ayıroğlu Sok 18 ■ (0212) 458 23 24 ■ www.cheerslighthouse. com ■ ₺
With a great location overlooking the Sea of Marmara and just downhill from the Hippodrome and Blue Mosque (see pp18–19), this hostel is great for those in search of a relaxed stay in the Old City on a budget.

Hotel Sultanahmet, Sultanahmet

MAP Q4 ■ Divanyolu Cad 20 ■ (0212) 527 02 39 ■ www.hotelsultanahmet. com ■ ₺
A popular budget choice on the main drag, the Sultanahmet does the basics well, with clean rooms and friendly staff.

Naz Wooden House Inn, Sultanahmet

MAP R6 ■ Akbıyık Değirmeni Sok 7 ■ (0212) 516 71 30 ■ www.naz woodenhouseinn.com ■ ₺

This wooden bed and breakfast is right in the heart of the Old City. The seven imaginatively decorated rooms are very good value, while the roof terrace has great views.

Peninsula

MAP G6 ■ Adliye Sok 6, Sultanahmet ■ (0212) 458 68 50 ■ www.hotel-peninsula.com ■ ₺

Well-located, this boutique hotel offers great value for money. There is a lovely roof terrace that also doubles up as the breakfast room. Service is excellent.

Şebnem Hotel, Sultanahmet

MAP S5 ■ Akbıyık Cad Adliye Sokak Çikmazı 1 ■ (0212) 517 66 23 ■ www.sebnemhotel. net ■ ₺

The Şebnem is a small, welcoming guesthouse, with 15 simple rooms (including one triple and one family room).

Side Hotel & Pension, Sultanahmet

MAP R5 ■ Utangaç Sok 20 ■ (0212) 517 22 82 ■ www.sidehotel.com ■ ₺

You can choose between a hotel room (half with air conditioning, half with fans), two self-catering apartments and a more basic pension (without air conditioning – all side by side, and under the same management. Close to Haghia Sophia (see pp16–17), with superb views from the roof.

World House Hostel

MAP F2 ■ Galipdede Cad 85, Galata ■ (0212) 293 55 20 ■ www.world houseistanbul.com ■ ₺

Set in a Genoese-style building dating from 1860, this large hostel offers a good mix of dorms, which can accommodate up to 14 people, and double rooms. Break-fast is included.

Agora Guest House and Hostel

MAP R5 ■ Amiral Tafdil Sok 6 ■ (0212) 458 55 47 ■ www.agoraguest house.com ■ ₺₺

The Agora blurs the lines between small budget hotel and hostel. There's a comfy communal living room/breakfast area, with computers, a huge TV and great terrace. Choose from mixed-sex dorms or private doubles.

Hotel Bulvar Palace, Aksaray

MAP D5 ■ Atatürk Bulvari 36 ■ (0212) 528 58 81 ■ www.hotelbulvarpalas. com ■ ₺₺

This is a great deal – a four-star hotel at a bar-gain price. The location near the Grand Bazaar is good, and the 70 rooms and 10 suites are well-equipped.

Manzara Istanbul, Galata

MAP F2 ■ Tatarbeyi Sok 26B ■ (0212) 252 46 60 ■ www.manzara-apartments.com ■ ₺₺

Located in the heart of the city, Manzara offers a wide range of stylish and spacious apartment options. Many have a balcony and terrace with breathtaking views over the Bosphorus.

Pasha Place

MAP J6 ■ Serdar-I Ekrem Cad, Galata ■ 07729 251 676 ■ www.istanbulplace. com ■ ₺₺

Pasha Place is the most prestigious property in the roster of Anglo-Turkish partnership Istanbul Place Apartments. Like most of their other loca-tions, it's a beautifully renovated 19th-century third-floor apartment located near the Galata Tower. This one offers two spacious double bed-rooms, one twin bedroom and a living room with views over the Golden Horn to the Old City, as well as a spacious kitchen, dining space and bar.

Bosphorus and Seafront Hotels

Anastasia Meziki Hotel (Princes' Islands)

MAP V6 ■ Malul Gazi Cad 24, Büyükada ■ (0216) 382 34 44 ■ www. mezikiotel.com ■ ₺

Arguably the most atmospheric hotel on the Büyükada island (see p99), this place oozes period charm with its turn of the 20th century Italianate style of architecture, original murals and antique furniture. Some rooms also have sea views.

Anzac Hotel, Çanakkale

Saat Kulesi Meydanı 8 ■ (0286) 217 77 77 ■ www. anzachotels.com ■ ₺

Travellers rave about the superb service at this small hotel, well-placed for Troy and Gallipoli. There are 25 rooms, a restaurant and rooftop bar (in summer).

Özdemir Pension (Princes' Islands)

MAP V6 ■ Ayyıldız Cad 41, Heybeliada ■ (0216) 351 18 66 ■ www.ozdemir pansiyon.org ■ ₺₺
Situated in the main settlement on Heybeliada *(see p99)* this inexpensive boarding house is perfect for a short stay. The friendly owner and staff are a plus.

Splendid Palace Hotel, Büyükada (Princes' Islands)

MAP V6 ■ 23 Nisan Cad 39 ■ (0216) 382 69 50 ■ www. splendidhotel.net ■ ₺₺
There are touches of Art Nouveau elegance in this very grand belle époque hotel, built in 1908 around a central courtyard. The 70 rooms and four suites all have balconies and wonderful views.

A'jia

MAP U2 ■ Çubuklu Cad 27, Kanlıca ■ (0212) 413 93 00 ■ www.ajiahotel. com ■ ₺₺₺
This is a lovely conversion of a traditional wooden waterfront *yalı* (mansion). A'jia is a little out of the city for some, but its mix of contemporary decor, informal ambience and luscious breakfast spreads in a peaceful location make it a winner.

Bosphorus Palace, Beylerbeyi (Asian side)

MAP U3 ■ Yalıboyu Cad 64 ■ (0216) 422 00 03 ■ www.bosphorus palace.com ■ ₺₺₺
Situated on the banks of the Bosphorus, this is the restored *yalı* (mansion) of a 19th-century Grand Vizier. With only 12 rooms, this intimate seaside hotel is romantic, making it perfect for couples. A private boat commutes to the centre.

Çırağan Palace Kempinski, Beşiktaş

MAP C4 ■ Çırağan Cad 32 ■ (0212) 326 46 46 ■ www.kempinski.com/ istanbul ■ ₺₺₺
Its terrace lapped by the Bosphorus, this Ottoman palace has a spa, health club and two of the city's best restaurants. Most of the 313 rooms are in the modern extensions, but for a real treat take one of the 11 suites in the original palace.

Four Seasons Bosphorus

Çırağan Cad 28, Beşiktaş ■ (0212) 381 40 00 ■ www.fourseasons. com/bosphorus ■ ₺₺₺
If you don't fancy the Four Seasons Sultanahmet in the touristy Old City, head for this one. The setting, in a restored 19th-century palace overlooking the famous strait is an ideal choice. There are also good spas, excellent restaurants and great views.

Grand Tarabya

MAP U2 ■ Haydar Aliyev Cad, Tarabya ■ (0212) 363 33 00 ■ www.thegrand tarabya.com ■ ₺₺₺
Out in the smart Bosphorus-front suburb of Tarabya (ancient Therapia) this hotel, right on a little bay of the famous strait, offers contemporary-styled rooms, good dining and a stunning spa with floor-to-ceiling glass windows that command stunning views over the Bosphorus.

Les Ottomans

MAP C4 ■ Muallim Naci Cad 68 ■ (0212) 359 15 00 ■ www.lesottomans.com ■ ₺₺₺
One of the city's most exclusive (and most expensive) hotels, Les Ottomans is housed in an old waterfront mansion and known for its architecture. Guests can admire superlative Bosphorus views, head down the strait on a hotel boat, unwind in the Caudalie spa or dine at Şamadan restaurant.

Shangri-La Bosphorus

MAP C5 ■ Hayrettin İskelesi Sk, Beşiktaş ■ (0212) 275 88 88 ■ www.shangri-la. com/Istanbul ■ ₺₺₺
Fashioned from an old tobacco factory this prestigious Bosphorus front hotel is made up of 186 rooms. Rooms are plush and suites have stunning views across to the Old City. As you might expect, Far Eastern (Cantonese) cuisine is a big feature here.

Sumahan on the Water, Çengelköy (Asian side)

MAP U3 ■ Kuleli Cad 43 ■ (0216) 422 80 00 ■ www.sumahan.com ■ ₺₺₺
Magnificently converted from an old *rakı* distillery by its architect owners, the 18-room Sumahan on the Asian shore of the Bosphorus is fast getting a reputation as one of Istanbul's best small hotels. Though not the best sightseeing base (although the hotel runs shuttle boats), it is ideal for couples on a romantic break.

For a key to hotel price categories see p112

General Index

Acknowledgments

Author

Melissa Shales is an award-winning travel writer, author, contributor or editor she has worked on more than 100 guide-books. She has written travel articles for many magazines, and was editor of Traveller magazine. During 2004–06 she was Chairman of the British Guild of Travel Writers.

The author would like to thank the following for their generosity, hard work and patience during the research of this book: the Turkish Tourist Office, particularly Joanna Marsh in London and Ilginay Altuntas in Istanbul; Emma Levine; and Victoria Gooch.

Additional contributor
Terry Richardson

Publishing Director Georgina Dee

Publisher Vivien Antwi

Design Director Phil Ormerod

Editorial Michelle Crane, Rachel Fox, Freddie Marriage, Fiodhna Ní Ghríofa, Scarlett O'Hara, Marianne Petrou, Sally Schafer,

Design Sunita Gahir, Bharti Karakoti

Cover Design Maxine Pedliham, Vinita Venugopal

Picture Research Phoebe Lowndes, Susie Peachey, Ellen Root, Oran Tarjan

Cartography Jasneet Arora, Suresh Kumar, Casper Morris, Simonetta Giori, Dominic Beddow

DTP Jason Little, George Nimmo

Production Linda Dare

Factchecker Terry Richardson

Proofreader Nikky Twyman

Indexer Helen Peters

Illustrator Chapel Design & Marketing

First edition created by Coppermill Books, London

Revisions Emma Brady, Sumita Khatwani, Shikha Kulkarni, Bandana Paul, Kanika Praharaj, Azeem Siddiqui, Aakanksha Singh, Priyanka Thakur, Stuti Tiwari

Commissioned Photography Christopher and Sally Gable, Rough Guides/Lydia Evans, Rough Guides/ Roger Mapp, Tony Souter, Clive Streeter, Francesca Yorke

Picture Credits
The publisher would like to thank the following for their kind permission to reproduce their photographs.

Key: a-above; b-below/bottom; c-centre; f-far; l-left; r-right; t-top

360istanbul: 53tr, 88crb.

4Corners: Sime/Anna Serrano 3tl, 24–5, 58–9; Sime/Stefano Scata 30–1.

Alamy Images: AgencyWestend61 GmbH/ Martin Siepmann 55bl; blickwinkel 74tl; David Coleman 21bl, 90tl; Ian G Dagnall 14cla; Digi.Log 46tl; Oguz Dikbakan 97tl; Mark Eveleigh 100bl; Godong 28bl; Tim Graham 73ctb; Hackenberg-Photo-Cologne 27ca; Have Camera Will Travel | Europe 45ctb; Chris Hellier 92br; Hemis.fr / Reza 55cla; Heritage Image Partnership Ltd/Fine Art Images *The capture of Constantinople by land and sea in 1204, Miniature from the Historia by William of Tyre,* 14&5 by Anonymous 38bl; imageBROKER/Martin Siepmann 98crb; JL Photography 33cr; Michael Kemp 20bl; ZUMA Press, Inc. 78d.

Ali Muhiddin Haci Bekir: 87br.

Aslıtane: 52tl, 79tr.

Bridgeman Images: National Gallery, London/ The Sultan Mehmet II (1480) by Gentile Bellini 39br.

Cembertitas Hamami: 30c.

Ciragan Palace Kempinski Istanbul, Laledan Restaurant: 95tr.

Corbis: Guido Cozzi 66cr; Monique Jaques 57b; Lebrecht Music & Arts 97cb; Hans Lippert 91br; Martin Siepmann 56l.

Dreamstime.com: 11geiserm 22clb; Alessandro0770 11tr; Steve Allen 10cl, 47ctb; Dejanns 54tr; Dbkg 11cb; Dinosmichail 40crb; Sergey Dzyuba 2tr, 36–7; Elenatur 14br; Evren Kalinbacak 77cla; Rodriguez Fontoba 72c; Giavara333 51cla; Nadiia Gerbish 47tr; Ihsan Gercelman 17cr, 17bl, 28cl, 40bc, 49ca; Gozlemne 51tr; Ozgur Guvenc 41bl, 82b; 99tl; Patricia Hofmeester 12br; Igdrzh 2tl, 8–9; Innaba18 41tr; Jackrezror 52clb; Jasmina 28–9, 35cr, 92tl, 94bl; Jim Kelcher 19bl; Khorunzha 50b; Teyana Kochneva 27br; Alessandra Lande 7cra; Madrugadaverde 22–3; Pavle Marjanovic 29bl; Luciano Mortula 12bl; Luba V Nel 22cl; Olha 26bc; Pepe14 23tr; Petitfrere 4cla, 33bc, 56crb; Marek Poplawski 71clb; Saaaaa 77bl; Saiko3p 34–5; 84bc; Sailorr 60tl, 80–1; Seajager 10crb, 18crb, 40tl, 75tr, 75b, 76l; Seryjig87 72tr; Siwssippo 17tl; Softdreams 12cl; Nikolai Sorokin 32bl; Mikhail Starodubov 13cr, Ssv94 3acrb; Tolga Tezcan 69tl, 98tl; Tinamou 10cla; Alexander Tolstykh 40bl; Tomas1111 70t; Vincentstithomas 93tl; Shuo Wang 16clb; Wedmoscow 51clb; Xantana 3tr, 102–3; Zastawkin 61tl; Minyan Zhou 7cr; Oleg Znamenskiy 4crb.

Four Seasons Hotel Istanbul at Sultanahmet: 67tr; Paul Thuysbaert 52bc.

Galata House: Bastiani 89cla.

Getty Images: Ayhan Altun 49b; Ullstein Bild 39tl; DeAgostini / *Sovereign Theodora and Antonina, Belisarius' wife, detail from Theodora with her entourage, mosaic, south wall of the apse, Basilica of San Vitale, Ravenna, Emilia-Romagna. Italy (6th century)* 41tr; Fuse 27tl; Heritage Images 29tl, /Fine Art Images/Pera Museum *Women Drinking Coffee* (1720s) by Jean-Baptiste Vanmour 15b, /Hulton Fine Art Collection/Pera Museum 15c; Angelika Hörschläger 26–7; Image Source 38tc; Izzet Keribar 54crb; Keystone 39cl; Yoray Liberman 55cla; Moment / DANNY HU 1; Winfield Parks 19crb; Tetra Images 16–7.

Giritli Restoran: 67clb.

Homer Books: 87tr.

Istanbul Archaeological Museum: 21cra.

Istanbul Modern: Muhsin Akgun 44tl; Murat Germen 91t.

Meze by Lemon Tree: 89br.

Nardis Jazz Club: Tasdemir Asan 88tl.

Pera Museum: 44cb; *Kaplumbağa Terbiyecisi (The Tortoise Trainer)* (1906) by Osman Hamdi Bey 85cla.

Robert Harding Picture Library: John Henry Claude 4cr; Eurasia 26bl; Stephen Rafferty 22br; Jose Fuste Raga 4b; Karl F. Schofmann 4clb, 32–3c, 33tl; Paul Seheult 4t; Tetra Images 6cla; Michael Zegers 4cl.

Sadberk Hanim Museum: 93bc.

Salon İKSV: aliguler 53bl.

Salt: 45tr.

Cover

Front and spine: **Getty Images:** DANNY HU.

Back: **Alamy Stock Photo:** isa özdere cla; **Dreamstime.com:** Badahos tr, Scaliger tl; **Getty Images:** Danny Hu b; **iStockphoto.com:** tunart crb.

Pull Out Map Cover

Getty Images: DANNY HU.

All other images © Dorling Kindersley
For further information see:
www.dkimages.com

As a guide to abbreviations in visitor information blocks: **Adm** = admission charge.

MIX
Paper from
responsible sources
FSC
www.fsc.org   FSC™ C018179

Penguin
Random
House

Printed and bound in China

First edition 2007

Published in Great Britain
by Dorling Kindersley Limited
80 Strand, London WC2R 0RL

Published in the United States by
DK US, 1450 Broadway, Suite 801
New York, NY 10018, USA

Copyright © 2007, 2020 Dorling
Kindersley Limited

A Penguin Random House Company

19 20 21 22 10 9 8 7 6 5 4 3 2 1

Reprinted with revisions 2009, 2011, 2013, 2015, 2016, 2020

ISSN 1479-344X
ISBN 978-0-2414-0775-2

SPECIAL EDITIONS OF DK TRAVEL GUIDES

DK Travel Guides can be purchased in bulk quantities at discounted prices for use in promotions or as premiums. We also offer special editions and personalized jackets, corporate imprints, and excerpts from all our books, tailored specifically to meet your needs.

To find out more, please contact:

in the US
specialsales@dk.com
in the UK
travelguides@uk.dk.com
in Canada
specialmarkets@dk.com
in Australia
penguincorporatesales@
penguinrandomhouse.com.au

Phrase Book

Pronunciation

Turkish uses a Roman alphabet of 29 letters:
8 vowels and 21 consonants. Letters that differ
from the English alphabet are: c, pronounced "j"
as in "jolly"; ç, pronounced "ch" as in "church"; ğ,
which lengthens the preceding vowel and is not
pronounced; ı, pronounced "uh"; ö, pronounced
"ur" (as in "further"); ş, pronounced "sh" as in "ship";
and ü, pronounced "ew" as in "few".

In an Emergency

English	Turkish	Pronunciation
Help!	İmdat	*eem-dat*
Call a doctor!	Bir doktor çağrın!	*beer dok-tor chah-ruhn*
Call an ambulance!	Bir ambulans çağırın!	*beer am-boo-lans chah-ruhn*
Call the police!	Polis çağrın!	*po-lees chah-ruhn*
Fire!	Yangın!	*yan-guhn*
Where is the nearest telephone/ hospital?	En yakın telefon/ hastane nerede?	*en ya-kuhn teh-leh-fon/ has-ta-neh neh-reh-deh*

Communication Essentials

English	Turkish	Pronunciation
Yes	Evet	*eh-vet*
No	Hayır	*h-eye-uhr*
Thank you	Teşekkür ederim	*teh-shek-kewr eh-deh-reem*
Please	Lütfen	*lewt-fen*
Excuse me	Affedersiniz	*af-feh-der-see-neez*
Hello	Merhaba	*mer-ha-ba*
Goodbye	Hoşça kalın	*hosh-cha Ka-luhn*
Morning	Sabah	*sa-bah*
Afternoon	Öğleden sonra	*ur-leh-den son-ra*
Evening	Akşam	*ak-sham*
Yesterday	Dün	*dewn*
Today	Bugün	*boo-gewn*
Tomorrow	Yarın	*ya-ruhn*
Here	Burada	*boo-ra-da*
There	Şurada	*shoo-ra-da*
What?	Ne?	*neh*
When?	Ne zaman?	*neh za-man*
Where?	Nerede?	*neh-reh-deh*

Useful Phrases

English	Turkish	Pronunciation
Pleased to meet you	Memnun oldum	*mem-noon ol-doom*
Where is/are?	Nerede?	*neh-reh-deh*
How far is it to?	Ne kadar uzakta?	*neh Ka-dar oo-zak-ta*
Do you speak English?	İngilizce biliyor musunuz?	*een-geel-eez-jeh bee-lee-yor moo-soo-nooz*
I don't understand	Anlamıyorum	*an-la-muh-yo-room*
Can you help me?	Bana yardım edebilir misiniz?	*ba-na yar-duhm eh-deh-bee-leer mee-see-neez*
I don't want	İstemiyorum	*ees-teh-mee-yo-room*

Useful Words

English	Turkish	Pronunciation
open	açık	*a-chuk*
bad	kötü	*kur-tew*
good/well	iyi	*iyi*
cold	soğuk	*soh-ook*
hot	sıcak	*suh-jak*
small	küçük	*kew-chewk*
big	büyük	*bew-yewk*

Shopping

English	Turkish	Pronunciation
How much is this?	Bu kaç lira?	*boo kach lee-ra*
I would like	İstiyorum	*ees-tee-yo-room*
Do you have?	Var mı?	*var muh*
Do you take credit cards?	Kredi kartı kabul ediyor musunuz?	*Kreh-dee kar-tuh ka-bool eh-dee-yor musunuz?*
What time do you open/ close?	Saat kaça açılıyor/ kapanıyor?	*Sa-at kach-a a-chuh-luh-yor/ ka-pa-nuh-yor*
this one	bunu	*boo-noo*
that one	şunu	*shoo-noo*
expensive	pahalı	*pa-ha-luh*
size (clothes)	beden	*beh-den*
size (shoes)	numara	*noo-mu-ra*
white	beyaz	*beh-yaz*
black	siyah	*see-yah*
red	kırmızı	*kuhr-muh-zuh*
yellow	sarı	*sa-ruh*
green	yeşil	*yeh-sheel*
blue	mavi	*ma-vee*
brown	kahverengi	*kah-veh-ren-gee*

Types of Shop

English	Turkish	Pronunciation
antiques shop	antikacı	*an-tee-ka-juh*
bakery	fırın	*fuh-ruhn*
bank	banka	*ban-ka*
bookshop	kitapçı	*kee-top-chuh*
cake shop	pastane	*pas-ta-neh*
chemist's/ pharmacy	eczane	*ej-za-neh*
greengrocer's	manav	*ma-nav*
leather shop	derici	*deh-ree-jee*
market/bazaar	çarşı/pazar	*char-shuh/pa-zar*
newsstand	gazeteci	*ga-zeh-teh-jee*
post office	postane	*pos-ta-neh*
shoe shop	ayakkabıcı	*eye-yak-Ka-buh-juh*
supermarket	süpermarket	*sew-per-mar-ket*
tailor	terzi	*ter-zee*
travel agency	seyahat acentesi	*seh-ya-hat a-jen-teh-see*

Sightseeing

English	Turkish	Pronunciation
castle	hisar	*hee-sar*
church	kilise	*kee-lee-seh*
mosque	cami	*ja-mee*
museum	müze	*mew-zeh*
palace	saray	*sar-eye*
park	park	*park*
square	meydan	*mey-dan*
information office	danışma bürosu	*da-nuhsh-mah bew-ro-soo*
Turkish bath	hamam	*ha-mam*

Transport

English	Turkish	Pronunciation
airport	havalimanı	*ha-va-lee-ma-nuh*
bus/coach	otobüs	*o-to-bewss*
bus stop	otobüs durağı	*o-to-bewss doo-ra-uh*

coach station	otogar	o-to-**gar**
mini bus	dolmuş	dol-**moosh**
fare	ücret	ewj-**ret**
ferry	vapur	va-**poor**
sea bus	deniz otobüsü	deh-**neez** o-to-**bew**-sew
station	istasyon	ees-tas-**yon**
taxi	taksi	tak-**see**
ticket	bilet	bee-**let**
ticket office	bilet gişesi	bee-**let** gee-sheh-**see**
timetable	tarife	ta-ree-**feh**

Staying in a Hotel

Do you have a vacant room?	Boş odanız var mı?	bosh o-da-**nuhz var** muh?
double room	iki kişilik bir oda	ee-**kee** kee-shee-**leek** beer o-**da**
twin room	çift yataklı bir oda	**cheeft** ya-tak-**luh** beer o-**da**
for one person	tek kişilik	**tek** kee-shee-**leek**
room with a bath	banyolu bir oda	**ban**-yo-loo beer o-**da**
shower	duş	doosh
porter	komi	ko-**mee**
key	anahtar	a-nah-**tar**
room service	oda servisi	o-**da** ser-vee-**see**
I have a reservation	Rezervas yonum var	reh-zer-vas-yo-**noom** var

Eating Out

I want to reserve a table	Bir masa ayırtmak istiyorum	beer **ma**-sa eye-uhrt-**mak** ees-**tee**-yo-room
The bill please	Hesap lütfen	heh-**sap** lewt-fen
I am a vegetarian	Et yemiyorum	et **yeh**-mee-yo-room
restaurant	lokanta	lo-**kan**-ta
waiter	garson	gar-**son**
menu	menü	men-**oo**
wine list	şarap listesi	sha-**rap** lees-teh-see
breakfast	kahvaltı	kah-val-**tuh**
lunch	öğle yemeği	ur-**leh** yeh-meh-**ee**
dinner	akşam yemeği	ak-**sham** yeh-meh-**ee**
starter	meze	**meh**-zeh
main course	ana yemek	a-**na** yeh-mek
dessert	tatlı	tat-**luh**
rare	az pişmiş	**az** peesh-meesh
well done	iyi pişmiş	ee-**yee** peesh-meesh
glass	bardak	bar-**dak**
bottle	şişe	shee-**sheh**
knife	bıçak	buh-**chak**
fork	çatal	cha-**tal**
spoon	kaşık	ka-**shuhk**

Menu Decoder

balık	ba-**luhk**	fish
bira	**bee**-ra	beer
bonfile	**bon**-fee-leh	fillet steak
buz	booz	ice
çay	ch-**eye**	tea
çorba	chor-**ba**	soup
dana eti	da-**na** eh-**tee**	veal
dondurma	don-door-**ma**	ice cream
ekmek	ek-**mek**	bread
et	et	meat
fırında	fuh-ruhn-**da**	roast
fıstık	fuhs-**tuhk**	pistachio nuts
gazoz	ga-**zoz**	fizzy drink
hurma	hoor-**ma**	dates
içki	eech-**kee**	alcohol
incir	een-**jeer**	figs
ızgara	uhz-**ga**-ra	charcoal-grilled

kahve	kah-**veh**	coffee
kara biber	ka-**ra** bee-ber	black pepper
karışık	ka-ruh-**shuhk**	mixed
kaymak	k-eye-**mak**	cream
kıyma	kuhy-**ma**	minced meat
köfte	kurf-**teh**	meatballs
kuzu eti	koo-**zoo** eh-**tee**	lamb
lokum	lo-**koom**	Turkish delight
maden suyu	ma-**den** soo-**yoo**	mineral water (fizzy)
meyve suyu	may-**veh** soo-**yoo**	fruit juice
midye	**meed**-yeh	mussels
patlıcan	pat-luh-**jan**	aubergine
peynir	pay-**neer**	cheese
pilav	pee-**lav**	rice
piliç	pee-**leech**	roast chicken
şarap	sha-**rap**	wine
şeker	sheh-**ker**	sugar
su	soo	water
süt	sewt	milk
tavuk	ta-**vook**	chicken
tereyağı	teh-**reh**-yah-uh	butter
tuz	tooz	salt
yoğurt	yoh-**urt**	yogurt
yumurta	yoo-moor-**ta**	egg
zeytinyağı	zay-**teen**-yah-uh	olive oil

Numbers

0	sıfır	**suh**-fuhr
1	bir	beer
2	iki	ee-**kee**
3	üç	ewch
4	dört	durt
5	beş	besh
6	altı	al-**tuh**
7	yedi	yeh-**dee**
8	sekiz	seh-**keez**
9	dokuz	doh-**kooz**
10	on	on
11	on bir	**on** beer
12	on iki	**on** ee-kee
13	on üç	**on** ewch
14	on dört	**on** durt
15	on beş	**on** besh
16	on altı	**on** al-tuh
17	on yedi	**on** yeh-dee
18	on sekiz	**on** seh-keez
19	on dokuz	**on** doh-kooz
20	yirmi	yeer-**mee**
21	yirmi bir	yeer-**mee beer**
30	otuz	o-**tooz**
40	kırk	kuhrk
50	elli	eh-**lee**
60	altmış	alt-**muhsh**
70	yetmiş	yet-**meesh**
80	seksen	sek-**sen**
90	doksan	dok-**san**
100	yüz	yewz
200	iki yüz	ee-**kee** yewz
1,000	bin	been
100,000	yüz bin	**yewz** been
1,000,000	bir milyon	**beer** meel-yon

Time

one minute	bir dakika	**beer** da-kee-ka
one hour	bir saat	**beer** sa-at
half an hour	yarım saat	ya-**ruhm** sa-at
day	gün	gewn
week	hafta	haf-**ta**
month	ay	eye
year	yıl	yuhl
Sunday	pazar	pa-**zar**
Monday	pazartesi	pa-**zar**-teh-see
Tuesday	salı	sa-**luh**
Wednesday	çarşamba	char-sham-**ba**
Thursday	perşembe	per-shem-**beh**
Friday	cuma	joo-**ma**
Saturday	cumartesi	joo-**mar**-teh-see

Street Index